Physical Characteristi...
Spinone Italiar...
(from the American Kennel Club

Back: The topline consists of two segments. The first slopes slightly downward in a nearly straight line...The second rises gradually and continues into a solid and well-arched loin. The underline is solid and should have minimal tuck up.

Croup: Well muscled, long...lightly rounded, well-filled-out croup.

Tail: Follows the line of the croup, thick at the base, carried horizontally or down. The tail should lack fringes.

Hindquarters: Thighs are strong and well muscled, stifles show good function...The hock...being ideal, is strong, lean and perpendicular to the ground.

Height: The height at the withers is 23 to 27 inches for males and 22 to 25 inches for females.

Coat: The ideal coat length is 1.5 to 2.5 inches on the body, with a tolerance of one-half inch over or under the ideal length. Head, ears, muzzle and front sides of legs and feet are covered by shorter hair. The coat is dense, stiff and flat or slightly crimped, but not curly, with an absence of undercoat.

Color: The accepted colors are: Solid white, white and orange; orange roan with or without orange markings; white with brown markings, brown roan with or without brown markings.

Spinone Italiano

By Richard Beauchamp

Contents

Training Your Spinone Italiano   **90**

Begin with the basics of training the puppy and adult dog. Learn the principles of house-training the Spinone Italiano, including the use of crates and basic scent instincts. Enter puppy kindergarten and introduce the pup to his collar and leash, and progress to the basic commands. Find out about obedience classes and other activities.

Healthcare of Your Spinone Italiano   **119**

By Lowell Ackerman DVM, DACVD
Become your dog's healthcare advocate and a well-educated canine keeper. Select a skilled and able veterinarian. Discuss pet insurance, vaccinations and infectious diseases, the neuter/spay decision and a sensible, effective plan for parasite control, including fleas, ticks and worms.

Showing Your Spinone Italiano   **144**

Step into the center ring and find out about the world of showing pure-bred dogs. Here's how to get started in AKC shows, how they are organized and what's required for your dog to become a champion. Take a leap into the realms of obedience trials, agility trials, tracking tests and field and hunting events.

KENNEL CLUB BOOKS® **SPINONE ITALIANO**
ISBN: 1-59378-307-8

Copyright © 2005 • Kennel Club Books, LLC
308 Main Street, Allenhurst, NJ 07711 USA
Cover Design Patented: US 6,435,559 B2 • Printed in South Korea

Photography by Alice van Kempen
with additional photographs by:

Paulette Braun, T.J. Calhoun, Alan and Sandy Carey, Carolina Biological Supply, Isabelle Français, Carol Ann Johnson, Bill Jonas, Dr. Dennis Kunkel, Tam C. Nguyen, Phototake and Jean Claude Revy.

Illustrations by Patricia Peters.

The publisher wishes to thank all of the owners whose dogs are illustrated in this book.

10 9 8 7 6 5 4 3 2 1

First and foremost a hunting dog, the Spinone Italiano is a reliable pointer, well suited to almost any terrain. He is an intuitive hunting companion with unending loyalty to his master.

SPINONE ITALIANO

ORIGIN OF THE BREED

Working side by side with your favorite canine hunting pal in the field or lounging with him in front of the fireplace reveals how well the dog has been integrated into our human lives. Certainly the last thing that picture would bring to mind is the wild ancestry that stands behind each and every dog, regardless of its size, purpose or country of origin. It is a well-established fact that, aided by various steps and crosses, all breeds of dog have descended from *Canis lupus*, the wolf, particularly from the branch of the family known as the Northern European Gray Wolf.

How long it took for the wolf to move out of the forest and into man's cave dwellings is a point of conjecture. However, it seems obvious that observing wolves in the hunt could easily have taught early man some survival techniques that he was able to use

BREED NAME

"Spinone" (singular) is pronounced *speh-no-nay*; the plural is spelled "Spinoni," not "Spinone," and is pronounced *speh-no-nee*.

advantageously. It goes without saying that the wolves that could assist man in satisfying his need for food would have been most highly prized. As the man-wolf relationship developed through the ages, certain descendants of these increasingly domesticated wolves began to assist in a myriad of capacities that ran from hauling to sounding the alarm when a marauding neighbor or beast of prey threatened.

Through the centuries, due to man's intervention and manipulation, many descendants of the original wolf stock underwent significant anatomical changes. In *The Natural History of Dogs*, authors Richard and Alice Feinnes trace the descendancy of all breeds of dog from one of four major groups, each of which traces back to separate and distinct branches of the wolf family. The four classifications are: the Dingo Group, the Greyhound Group, the Northern Group and the Mastiff Group.

Each of the groups has its own

> **ANCIENT DOG GROUPS**
> As early as the first century AD, Romans had classified dogs into six general groups: House Guardian Dogs, Shepherd Dogs, Sporting Dogs, War Dogs, Scent Dogs and Sight Dogs. Most dogs we know today can trace their ancestry directly back to dogs from these groups. A good many other breeds were developed by combining two or more individuals from those original groups to create yet another "breed."

particular characteristics that have been handed down through countless generations to our modern dog. These characteristics have become the features that individualize and specialize our pure-bred dogs of the day. As we trace back into the history of man's hunting companions, we find a common denominator in the Mastiff Group. This group owes its primary heritage to the Tibetan wolf (*Canis lupus chanco* or *laniger*). The great diversity of the dogs included in this group indicates that they were not entirely of pure blood, as many of the specific breeds undoubtedly were influenced by descendants of the other three groups. The descendants of the Mastiff Group are widely divergent but are known to include many of the scenting breeds. These are the breeds that find game by the use of

In the 14th through 16th centuries, the Spinone Italiano was popular with various European courts, accompanying noblemen to the hunt and performing admirably in the field.

their olfactory senses rather than by sight, which is to say that they rely upon their noses rather than their eyes. They include the breeds we now classify as gundogs and the true hounds, or scenthounds.

As man became more sophisticated and his lifestyle more complex, he learned that these descendants of the wolf could be bred in such a manner as to suit his specific needs. Often these needs were based on the manner in which man himself went after game and the terrain in which he was forced to do so. The importance here is that man had taken control of the individual dogs that mated. Particular characteristics were prized and inbreeding practices employed to perpetuate these characteristics.

One type of hunting dog that man developed retained the wolf characteristics of pursuing the prey until it was cornered and killed, until it was chased up a tree or until the dog gave up in exhaustion. This practice is more or less typical of that group of dogs known today as the hounds. While the tenacity was held in high regard, a hound's willingness to chase could continue on for miles if need be, and some men found keeping up rather tiresome.

Thus was born a need for the hunting dog that never followed through with the chase or the attack. Its job was not to do the hunting or killing, but rather to

CANIS LUPUS

"Grandma, what big teeth you have!" The gray wolf, a familiar figure in fairy tales and legends, has had its reputation tarnished and its population pummeled over the centuries. Yet it is the descendants of this much-feared creature to which we open our homes and hearts. Our beloved dog, *Canis domesticus*, derives directly from the gray wolf, a highly social canine that lives in elaborately structured packs. In the wild, the gray wolf can range from 60 to 175 pounds, standing between 25 and 40 inches in height.

assist the human hunter by finding the game and indicating its discovery to the hunter quietly so as not to scare away the game. Further, like any good assistant, the hunting dog obeyed its master's commands without hesitation.

References have been made to the existence of this kind of dog as early as the time of the ancient Greeks. Written records point to the existence of a rough-coated breed of dog in Italy that signaled their discovery of game by assuming a rigid position and placing their bodies in direct line with the find, thus directing the

THE POINTING BREEDS OF EUROPE

Great Britain	Pointer
France	Braque d'Auvergne, Braque d'Ariége, Braque du Bourbonnais, Braque Dupuy, Braque Français, Braque St. Germain, Korthals
Spain	Perdiguero de Burgos, Perdiguero Navarro
Portugal	Perdigueiro Portugues
Germany	Weimaraner, Pudelpointer, Stichelhaar, German Shorthaired Pointer, German Wirehaired Pointer (Drahthaar)
Italy	Bracco Italiano, Spinone Italiano
Belgium	Braque Belge
Denmark	Hertha Pointer, Gamle Dansk
Czech Republic	Cesky Fousek
Slovak Republic	Dalmatian
Hungary	Vizsla

Braque du Bourbonnais.

Pointer.

Braque St. Germain.

Perdiguero de Burgos.

Perdigueiro Portugues.

Braque d'Auvergne.

Bracco Italiano.

Cesky Fousek.

Braque Français.

Two Italian hunting breeds, the Bracco Italiano with his Spinone countryman.

hunter to the hiding place. Although most people are inclined to think of a pointer as a distinct breed of dog, the name actually refers to an entire group of dogs that work the field in a distinctive manner, not unlike that described by the ancient Greeks.

Countries throughout Europe developed their own unique breeds of "pointer" or "pointing dog" based on the demands made by the terrain of their respective locales. The results of these efforts can be seen in such breeds as Germany's Shorthaired Pointer, the Braque Français of France, the breed known simply as the Pointer, which was the UK's contribution, and Italy's Bracco Italiano and Spinone Italiano.

The Italian pointers were particularly popular with royalty across Europe in the 14th through 16th centuries. The royal courts rode horseback to the hunt, and good-sized, long-legged dogs suited the occasion well.

Mery was a Best of Breed winner from the early 1930s, a time when the Spinone Italiano was known solely as a working dog and was a rarity in the show ring.

Controversy exists regarding the root source of the Italian pointing breeds, but one important source of the breed's history is Fiorenzo Fiorone's *The Encyclopedia of Dogs*, written in collaboration with the Fédération Cynologique Internationale (FCI). The book was first published in Italy as *Enciclopedia del Cane* in 1970. Fiorone's work was closely supervised by Italian breed authorities and is particularly commended by Giulio Colombo, one of the National Association of Italian Dog Fanciers' (NAIDF) most active and highly respected presidents.

Fiorone appears to be most

closely in agreement with Tschudy's study, which indicates that the Spinone was developed in Italy during the Roman era, with its origins in coarse-haired setters brought there by Greek traders and others from the western Adriatic coast in ancient times. These setters were crossbred with a white Mastiff-type dog already prevalent along the coasts of Italy at the time. The results were called Spinoni.

Accurate representation of the working Spinone Italiano appeared in Italian art as early as the 1400s. It should be noted that it was the working ability of the breed that was of primary consequence and what caused the breed to be held in high esteem by Italian sportsmen even then. Paramount concern has been the preservation of these natural abilities. There is no doubt that various strains and deviations existed throughout Italy in the centuries that followed, but there is also fairly unanimous agreement that the dogs also shared many common characteristics.

It appears, even in the initial attempts to define the essence of

the Spinone Italiano, that certain characteristics were described that have remained constant through the years. Head characteristics, the breed's unique silhouette, the quality of the skin and rough coat texture, along with large size, continue as the traits necessary to the breed's correct conformation and appearance.

The name of the breed has evolved alongside the development of the breed itself. First called Bracco Spinoso (Prickly Pointer), and Bracco Spinone later, finally in 1887 it was decided to call the breed simply Spinone Italiano. The exact translation of "Spinone" in English is, in fact, "very prickly." Some say the name describes the quality of the coat. Still others believe the name indicates the type of ground upon which the dogs work so

The tail of the Spinone Italiano is docked at birth. Shown here with docked (LEFT) and undocked (RIGHT) tails.

FAMILY HISTORY
There are breeders in Italy whose families have maintained Spinone Italiano lines that trace as far back as the 16th century. These individuals have been highly successful in both hunting and show-ring endeavors.

A Spinone
Italiano at work.
The rough coat
protects the dog
no matter the
terrain.

efficiently—ground thickly
overgrown with every kind of
dense prickly bush.

A definitive standard for the
breed was written in 1939 by
Giuseppe Solaro. This standard
remained basically unaltered until
1944 when it was modified by the
governing body for all pure-bred
dog activities in Italy, Ente
Nationale della Cinofilia Italiano
(ENCI).

The two World Wars did little
to assist or even maintain the
development of the Spinone
Italiano, but, at the close of World
War II, devoted breed fanciers
gathered the remaining specimens
of the breed and planned careful
breedings to eliminate the undesirable qualities contributed by
unfortunate crosses to other
breeds. Great credit must go to the

members of the Italian breed club,
La Famiglia dello Spinoni, for the
breed's renaissance. Formed in
1950, the organization was given
recognition by the ENCI as the
official breed club in Italy. The
name of the club has since been
changed to Club Italiano Spinoni
(CISp).

**THE SPINONE ITALIANO
IN ENGLAND**
There is little doubt but also little
documentation of the importation
of Spinoni into Britain throughout
the early years of the 20th century.
Attempts to establish the breed,
however, went unrewarded. Then,
late in the 1950s, the internation-
ally famous concert pianist Alberto
Semprini brought a pair of Spinoni
named "Arno" and "Gita" with
him when he toured the UK. The

pair was housed at Ryslip Kennels from 1957 to 1958 and during that time Gita whelped a litter. England's Kennel Club paved the way for future imports to be registered by placing Arno and Gita on the Breed Register.

Over 20 years later, in 1981, Mrs. Mary Moore (Odivane) and Dr. Ruth Tattersall (Westoy) imported four of the breed into the UK. The imports were a male, Friz del Odivane, and the litter sisters Clara and Megana dei Marchesi dei Galpiott from Odivane. The trio was from Sergio Cantoni's kennel in northern Italy. Dr. Tattersall's female named "Lidia" came from the same kennel. This time interest in the breed flourished. All three of the bitches imported from Sergio Cantoni's kennel were bred, but Megana's two litters by Friz are

Although still considered a rare breed, Spinoni are becoming more well known world-wide. This quality example hails from the Netherlands.

those that had the greatest impact and are credited as becoming the cornerstone of the breed in the UK.

The Italian Spinone Club of Great Britain (ISCGB) was organized through the efforts of many breed diehards including Dr.

Spinone Italiano from the UK, where the breed has only been truly established since the latter half of the 20th century.

Tattersall, Glenys Barlow (Wintercleugh), Cyndy and Malcolm Bevan (Snowlodge), Margaret and John Curgenven (Chruston), Jean Houltram (Caldocani), Viv Rosser (Nantiderri), Lorraine Spencer (Bannonbrig), Gael Stenton (Gaesten) and Helen Thomson (Deldawn).

Initially entered and shown in rare-breed competition, the Spinone Italiano made rapid headway, recording impressive wins in that category as early as 1986. Linda Collins's Sacul Romeo Rio of Wynsett and Rio's granddaughter, Gallowdyke Pawnee, owned by Mike Gadsby and her breeders Sheila and John Piggin, both achieved the Best

Photo circa 1932, published in *Hutchinson's Dog Encyclopedia*. Part of the caption read: "Spinone Italiano. Intelligent, intrepid and untiring, this is undoubtedly the most popular with sportsmen in its native country." The caption also acknowledged the Italian breeders for reviving the breed from near-extinction.

Rare Breed in Show distinction. Rio was Top-Winning Rare Breed Dog for 1986.

The ISCGB held its first Open Show in 1989. Topping the entry was Mrs. Collins's Sacul Romeo Rio of Wynsett, with Best Puppy in Show being awarded to Mr. and Mrs. Shimell's Connomar Careena. The year 1994 proved to be a banner year for the breed—the Spinone Italiano became eligible to receive Challenge Certificates (CCs). The efforts of the breed's many staunch supporters were finally rewarded.

The first Show Champion was Gallowdyke Wreckless Eric at Sundeala who, after winning his first two CCs at Crufts and the Scottish Kennel Club, acquired the title at ISCGB's first championship event in June 1994. Eric was owned by Barbara Davies and Michael Gadsby and bred by John and Sheila Piggin and Michael Gadsby.

Dedicated breed fanciers began to express some concern over the fact that the Spinone Italiano, though widely used throughout Europe as a hunting dog, was not receiving the field trial support that the breed warranted in the UK. Thus a sigh of relief was released when Sh. Ch. Sentling Zenzero achieved his Gundog Working Certificate at the German Wirehaired Pointer Club's novice field trial in December 1998. In so doing, Zenzero became Britain's first Champion Spinone Italiano. The achievement was particularly noteworthy in that Zenzero, among his many outstanding victories, also claimed first in the Gundog Group at Birmingham National and Best in Show at the breed club championship show under judge Penny Robertson. He completed 1998 as the Top-Winning Spinone Italiano. Zenzero is regularly worked during the shooting season by his owners, Liz and Jonathan Shaw, who bred him. He was whelped in April 1994 in a litter by Wynsett Jumpin' Jack Flash *ex* Sentling Ancona. Ancona's litter brother, Italian Sh. Ch. Sentling Affidato, is the only UK-bred Spinone Italiano to win a title in the breed's home country.

Meanwhile, in Italy, the fanciers of the breed have expressed wonder at the fact that the breed is referred to as the Italian Spinone in England. In an article written for *Dog News* by Italian breed authority and judge Dr. G. W. Mentasti, he states, "To start with, we must define the name of the breed: Spinone, not Spinone Italiano. In the FCI list there is only one Spinone, and only one breed with Spinone characteristics. So, there is really no need to add further adjectives."

Nonetheless, the fact remains that the breed is known throughout the UK as the Italian Spinone and in the US as the Spinone Italiano. It is highly

A handsome pair of modern-day Spinone Italiano from the UK.

doubtful that any change in the name will occur, as there are many breeds in the UK that are happily burdened by superfluous adjectives (Hungarian Vizsla, Australian Silky Terrier, Japanese Shiba Inu, etc.).

Bedecked by his many awards is Ch. Rufus Di Morghengo MH, owned by Lena Amirian.

THE SPINONE IN THE US
By Jan Naigus

Although the Spinone Italiano is still considered by many to be a "new" breed in the United States, it is known that a Spinone arrived in this country in 1903. Nothing more is known about that dog or any others until nearly 30 years later. In 1931 a Dr. Gigante imported a pair of Spinoni from Italy. Together with a barber, whose name has been lost, he periodically imported Spinoni from Italy and established a breeding program that lasted until 1958. At that time the dogs were sold, and there are no records of what happened to them. Spinoni remained little known for many years.

A Spinone was entered in the Westminster Kennel Club Dog Show in the Miscellaneous Class in 1932 and 1933, and an entry in *Hutchinson's Dog Encyclopedia* (1934) states, "Spinoni are workers and are, therefore, seldom seen in the show ring. [A] remarkably fine specimen, however, was exhibited by Mr. Emil Perona at the Westminster Kennel Club show at Madison Square Gardens, New York, where it was judged to be the best Spinone Italiano in the show, 'Mery'." After 1933, no Spinone would be seen at Westminster until 2001, when the breed was officially recognized by the American Kennel Club (AKC).

In 1970 a Spinone club was founded in Alabama, but was discontinued after a short time. Then, in the 1980s, a common interest in hunting and in the Spinone brought together four men who, though not close geographically, would meet and establish the Spinone Club of America (SCOA) in 1987. Paolo Sacchetti (Del Sasso) had brought Spinoni with him when he came to the US from Italy; Larry Dickey (Ruff Creek) obtained a Spinone, Alba del Sasso, from Paolo; Larry contacted Jim Channon (Risky Business) after noticing a North American Versatile Hunting Dog Association (NAVHDA) registration of a Spinone that belonged to Jim; and Jim had gotten his Spinoni from Canadian Guido Malandruccolo (Di Morghengo). Three dogs from those early days can be said to be the foundation of

Ch. Risky Business Pistol's Fire CD, JH, bred by Jim Channon and owned by the Applegates and Junior McDaniel, won the national specialty in 2004.

Ch. Rufus Di Morghengo MH, owner-handled by Lena Amirian, winning the breed at Westminster Kennel Club in 2004.

the breed in the US: Nico Del Benaco at Risky Business, a white and orange dog imported from Italian breeder Valentino Vignola; Iso Dell'Adige, a brown roan dog, also from Italy, bred by Mr. Bonvicini; and Deldawn Federico at Dazen, a white and orange dog bred by Helen Thompson of England. The majority of American-bred Spinoni trace back to these three dogs.

A primary purpose of the SCOA was to foster, improve, encourage and promote the Spinone as a hunting dog in North America. From the beginning, annual meetings were held that featured hunting tests and a conformation show as well as the annual club business meeting. The club maintained a registry of Spinoni in the US, and later oversaw the recognition of the Spinone Italiano by the American Kennel Club. The SCOA was officially recognized as the AKC parent club for the Spinone Italiano on February 11, 2000, and the Spinone was accepted into the Sporting Group on September 27, 2000.

The first AKC champion and top-winning Spinone for that year was Ch. Mals-About Little

Ch. Cerebella del Caos JH, CGC, owned by Debbie Perrott, winning the breed at Westminster.

Drummer Boy, bred, owned and handled by Pat Fendley. After AKC recognition, the first official SCOA national specialty show was held in April 2001 in Hustle, Virginia. Winning the breed and finishing his championship that day was Rufus Di Morghengo, bred by Guido Malandruccolo and owned and handled by Lena Amirian. Best of Opposite Sex was Ch. Cerebella del Caos, bred by Allison Schultz and owned by Debbie Perrott. Best in Sweepstakes was Isis La Dolce Vita, bred and owned by Jan Naigus. Cerebella was also the first Spinone Best of Breed winner at the Westminster Kennel Club show in 2001. Rufus went on to repeat his national specialty win in 2003 and won the breed at Westminster in 2004.

The first Spinone to win Best in Show at an all-breed show was Ch. Dee Tias Julius Pleaser JH, bred by Chuck Gern and owned by Michelle and Lauren Brustein and Dave Brooks. Julius was also the national specialty winner in 2002 and the winner of the breed at Westminster in 2005.

The versatility of the Spinone is exemplified by the dogs' successes in the field, the conformation ring and the obedience ring. Rufus, the first specialty winner, went on to earn a Master Hunter title in AKC tests and has the distinction of being the first Spinone to earn a NAVHDA

Versatile Championship. Ch. Cerebella del Caos JH, CGC earned her Junior Hunter title.

Ch. Dee Tias Julius Pleaser JH prized in the NAVHDA Natural Ability test as well as earning his Junior Hunter title. Ch. Risky Business Pistol's Fire CD, JH, bred by Jim Channon and owned by Ed and Suzanne Applegate and Junior McDaniel, not only earned her Junior Hunter title but also finished her Companion Dog obedience title the same day she won the SCOA national specialty for the second time. Another notable dog is Ed Hanna's Risky Business Nita, bred by Jim Channon. Nita was the first Spinone to compete in the NAVHDA Invitational Test, and although she did not qualify that first trip, Ed and Nita kept training and earned another invitation. This time Nita received her Versatile Championship with the maximum score possible, the only Spinone to do so and an accomplishment few dogs can match.

Ch. Dee Tias Julius Pleaser JH, owned by Michelle and Lauren Brustein and Dave Brooks, is a multiple Best in Show winner.

Spinone registrations have experienced substantial growth in the first years since AKC recognition, and, while still considered one of the more rare breeds, the Spinone is now regularly seen in the show ring and hunting tests and is known as a wonderful companion dog as well. Americans devoted to the breed hope that the Spinone will not lose its status as a "well-kept secret" and become too popular, risking overbreeding and the loss of the characteristics that endear the breed to its fanciers.

SPINONE ITALIANO

There is probably nothing quite so captivating as a comical little Spinone Italiano puppy with his floppy ears, gangly legs and sweet expression. If you haven't fully decided whether or not to add a Spinone Italiano puppy to your life, a visit to the home or kennel where there is a litter of puppies is probably *not* the best idea in the world. Anyone even thinking of dog ownership is going to be hard-pressed to resist these prickly Italian charmers.

For this very reason, the person who anticipates owning a Spinone Italiano must give serious thought to the final decision. All puppies are cute and cuddly, and Spinone Italiano puppies are certainly no exception. Puppies are charming and seductive, but puppies are living, breathing and very adventurous little creatures. Not only that, they depend entirely upon their human owners for everything once they leave their mother and littermates.

BEFORE YOU BUY
Careful consideration is crucial regardless of which breed you might be considering. However, there are special considerations for those who might be thinking about bringing a Spinone Italiano puppy into their lives.

Firstly, the Spinone Italiano is a hunting dog. The breed was created to hunt, and centuries have been invested in cultivating and developing the breed's hunting characteristics. The Spinone Italiano's mental and physical development depends upon his being given the opportunity to exercise the mental and physical characteristics that he has inherited.

The Spinone Italiano needs room to run fast and long and over all kinds of terrain. He must be given opportunity to smell the smells, hear the sounds and see the creatures in nature that will stimulate all of the characteristics that his ancestors have passed down to him. These needs cannot be satisfied by a walk around the block a few times a week!

If not given these opportunities, the Spinone Italiano puppy can become a frustrated adolescent who vents these frustrations in ways that will make you regret ever having considered dog ownership. Is the dog being impossible and incorrigible? No!

The dog is simply following his nature, which demands that he put his incomparable energy level to good use.

Failure to think ahead and understand the amount of time and readjustment that dog ownership involves is one of the primary reasons that there are so many abandoned canines whose lives end in animal-rescue centers and shelters. Buying a dog, especially a puppy, before someone is absolutely sure he wants to make that commitment can be a grave mistake.

Before a person decides to buy a dog, there are some very basic conditions that must be considered. One of the first significant questions that must be answered is whether or not the person who will actually be given the responsibility of the dog's care actually wants a dog—particularly a dog that demands the level of outdoor action that the Spinone Italiano requires. This may sound like a moot point, but wanting a dog and wanting to care for it properly do not necessarily go hand in hand.

Children are often wildly enthusiastic about having a dog. Parents are often easily persuaded, given that most people recognize that pets are a wonderful method of teaching children responsibility. It should be remembered, however, that childhood enthusiasm can inspire a youngster to promise anything

HEART-HEALTHY
In this modern age of ever-improving cardio-care, no doctor or scientist can dispute the advantages of owning a dog to lower a person's risk of heart disease. Studies have proven that petting a dog, walking a dog and grooming a dog all show positive results toward lowering your blood pressure. The simple routine of exercising your dog—going outside with the dog and walking, jogging or playing catch—is heart-healthy in and of itself. If you are normally less active than your physician thinks you should be, adopting a dog may be a smart option to improve your own quality of life as well as that of another creature.

to get what he wants...but that same enthusiasm may wane very quickly. Further, today's children have extremely busy schedules with homework, extra-curricular activities and social events. Who will take care of the puppy once the novelty wears off and, again, does that person want a dog?

Desire to own a dog aside, does the lifestyle of the family actually provide for responsible dog ownership? If the entire family is away from early morning to late at night, who will provide for all of the puppy's needs? Feeding, sufficient exercise time, outdoor access and the like cannot be provided if no one is home.

Another important factor to consider is whether or not this breed of dog is suitable for the person or the family with whom it will be living. A full-grown Spinone Italiano can handle the rough-and-tumble play of young children, though a puppy cannot. A very young Spinone Italiano puppy should only be allowed playtime with young children when adults are present to supervise. The very young Spinone Italiano puppy can be dropped or injured unintentionally by children unable to properly hold or carry the puppy. On the other hand, the rapidly growing Spinone Italiano puppy has no idea of his size or strength and could easily upend and

FAMILY DEVOTION

There is no doubt that the trait endearing the Spinone Italiano to the many families that own the breed is his devotion to the entire family. This is particularly so in regard to the children of the family. Even well-behaved toddlers find the adult Spinone Italiano to be a willing and patient playmate who can even be relied upon to invent games if need be to keep a child amused.

injure a toddler by accident.

The grooming of an adult Spinone Italiano doesn't require as much time and patience as do the luxuriously coated breeds, but that does not mean the breed needs no grooming—on the contrary! The owner must commit to keeping the Spinone Italiano's coat in good condition, free of mats, tangles, burs and pesky parasites.

As great as claims are for a Spinone Italiano's adaptability and intelligence, remember there is no dog, no matter what breed, that doesn't need to be taught every household rule that must be observed. Some dogs learn more quickly than others, and puppies are just as inclined to forget or disregard lessons as are human children.

OPPOSITE: If the Spinone Italiano is properly introduced, and the children are instructed in the proper handling of the dog, a wonderful relationship usually develops.

The sweet, pleading expression of the Spinone Italiano is one of the breed's most endearing features.

WHY A PURE-BRED DOG?

It is almost impossible to determine what a mixed-breed puppy will look like as an adult. More importantly, it is impossible to determine what the temperament of a puppy of mixed parentage is going to be like. Will he be suitable for the person or family who wishes to own him? If the puppy grows up to be too big, too hairy or too active for the owner, what then will happen to him?

Size and temperament can vary to a degree, even within pure-bred dogs. Still, controlled breeding over many generations has produced dogs giving us reasonable assurance of what a pure-bred puppy will look and act like when he reaches maturity. This predictability is more important than one might think.

Just about any dog whose background is made up of sound and sane individuals has the potential to be a loving companion. However, the predictability of a pure-bred dog offers reasonable insurance that he will suit not only the owner's esthetic and personality demands but also the owner's lifestyle.

Before you bring a Spinone Italiano puppy into your household, visit breeders and spend as much time with both puppies and adults as you can. You must confirm that the adult Spinone Italiano is the dog that appeals to you esthetically and temperamentally, and above all be certain that you will in fact be a suitable owner for the breed.

CHARACTER OF THE SPINONE ITALIANO

The Spinone Italiano—puppy or adult—has the sweetest, most beguiling expression that you can find on any breed of dog. Thus it is all the more surprising to find the lengths to which the Spinone Italiano will go to accomplish his ends—particularly so if those ends involve food! A Spinone Italiano is always hungry—morning, noon and night. The fact that he's just had his dinner is no deterrent. If food is nearby, your

ENERGY AND ENDURANCE

The Spinone Italiano has a genetic predisposition to hunt and the high energy level that is required to perform well. This is not to be confused with a "hyper" or "frenetic" personality but is rather an expression of the great energy and endurance levels that have been enhanced through centuries of selected breeding. However, given sufficient exercise, the Spinone Italiano can act simultaneously as an outstanding field dog and a loving and devoted family member.

Spinone Italiano wants it! Spinoni are clever to a fault and can work out ways to get into and out of any cupboard or enclosure that would be entirely foolproof to most other breeds—even if it means eating through what stands between him and the snack he's after.

Immediately after food on the Spinone Italiano's list of favorite things, or perhaps even right alongside of it, is the breed's love of the outdoors and being put to work in the capacity for which the breed was created—hunting! And when speaking of hunting, it cannot be stressed enough that a Spinone Italiano is first and foremost a hunting dog. Are there Spinoni that are bred just to be pets? Not by people who truly love the breed!

The desire and the ability to hunt are what have allowed the Spinone Italiano to flourish throughout its history. Most Spinoni Italiano show dogs are dad's "hunting pal" on Saturday and mom and the children's show dog on Sunday. People who love the Spinone Italiano would have it no other way.

Spinoni are listed among the most intelligent of all breeds of dog, a distinction that is both good and bad—good in that they can learn just about anything you want to teach them, but bad in that a Spinone Italiano can become bored very easily without activities that keep him mentally and physically busy. The Spinone Italiano is not a breed that can be left on its own continuously or kept outdoors without another canine companion. The breed's long-standing history of working

Even the ever-active Spinone Italiano needs to take a break from time to time!

alongside man and other dogs in the field has made the Spinone Italiano a very social creature. Denied the opportunity to be with those he loves, the Spinone Italiano will demand attention by developing behavioral problems. Destructive digging, chewing and barking are usually signs of a bored Spinone Italiano.

The Spinone Italiano is an ideal family dog in that he is able to share his devotion with every member of the family and has an innate ability to adjust his own mood to that of whatever family member he is with. He will sound the alarm to alert the family to the approach of a stranger but will be delighted to greet that same stranger if given assurance that all is well.

TRAINABILITY OF THE BREED
Life is indeed the proverbial "bowl of cherries" to the Spinone Italiano, and, admittedly, the young dog may appear to be more

> **SIZE DIFFERENCES**
> Both male and female Spinoni make excellent companions and work equally well in the field. Their primary difference is in height and weight. Recommended size for males is 23–27 inches and 76–85 pounds. Females should be between 22–25 inches and 61–75 pounds.

than just a bit silly. However, do not mistake these characteristics for stupidity. On the contrary, this is an extremely clever breed that is prone to study your every action and reaction. Should you not establish the fact that you indeed are the pack leader early on, expect your Spinone Italiano to try his hand at it! By and large, the breed is very amiable, and there is no reason for the breed to be anything else unless you provide the circumstances.

There are times when your Spinone needs correction, and you must be forthright and uncompromising in this respect. This, however, never means you should resort to striking your dog. A rap on the nose with a finger or holding his head in your hands with eye-to-eye contact and a stern "No!" may be necessary and will not shatter the Spinone Italiano, but harsh methods can destroy the dog's spirit and trainability.

Repetition and determination work best with the breed, and,

A Spinone Italiano likes to keep busy—and if not otherwise occupied, you can be sure he'll find something to do!

once learned, lessons seem almost a natural part of the Spinone Italiano's character. Avoidance of bad habits works best. Not allowing unwanted behavior to occur in the first place is infinitely simpler than trying to convince your Spinone Italiano pup to stop something he has been doing all along.

Those who work with the Spinone Italiano in the field are quick to say that, once trained, the Spinone Italiano does not forget. He is a ready and willing hunter who is happy to work almost any terrain from the mountains to a pond but, at his very best, penetrating dense growth and underbrush. The working Spinone Italiano has great endurance and tolerance for both heat and cold. He maintains excellent contact skills while working and is a prompt and dependable retriever.

SPINONI AND THE WORLD AT LARGE

Spinoni love their masters and their normally happy-go-lucky manner belies a protective instinct that emerges when something unusual occurs. This he handles by sounding the alarm—barking. Some Spinoni become completely enthralled with the sound of their own voices and entertain themselves by barking for no other reason than they enjoy it. Not a good idea unless you and your Spinone Italiano live in

COLORS

Although one is more likely to see a predominance of solid white and white and orange Spinoni at dog shows, the breed is found in brown roan and orange roan coloration as well. Those colors as well as white with brown markings are equally acceptable according to the breed standard and therefore in the show ring. Preference is strictly on the part of the beholder.

some remote part of a forest!

Although you undoubtedly will want to be forewarned with the arrival of a stranger, the warning doesn't have to continue *ad infinitum*. After a few barks, praise and pet your dog. This will usually make him pause—briefly. Once he attempts to begin barking again, like most any Spinone Italiano will, say "No!" immediately. It will take some persistence on your part, but eventually you will get your message through.

OTHER PETS AND ANIMALS

Some Spinoni are a bit reserved when strange dogs approach; others know no enemies in the canine world. Most properly raised Spinoni are happy to coexist with any other four-legged family pet that might share the home. Winged pets and rodents will have little problem with a Spinone Italiano as long as they are confined to their cages. Everything in a Spinone Italiano's genetic makeup tells the dog something must be done about these little critters when they are loose. It will take a good deal of restraint for a Spinone Italiano to remain calm and indifferent with the family parakeet or hamster darting about the room.

All hunting dogs have the chase instinct, and if your cat or resident dog will be inclined to bolt at the sight of this new intruder, it is best to keep your Spinone Italiano on his leash. If the relationship begins with the chase, it will take a lot of doing to break the resident animal's hasty retreat and your Spinone Italiano's willingness to pursue. Give them time to become acquainted and trust each other before they are free to interact on their own.

HEALTH CONCERNS

It is not the least bit unusual to have the well-bred and well-cared-for Spinone Italiano live to be 12 years old, and there are many cases of individuals living to be 14 years of age and in relatively good health. Since your Spinone Italiano puppy will be living with you for many, many years, you want those years to be enjoyable ones in which your dog leads a happy, healthy life. Like other breeds of dog, there are

ADOPTING AN ADULT

Adopting an adult Spinone Italiano can be a good choice for an adult or elderly person who wishes to avoid the trials of puppyhood. It should be understood that, like any adult, the mature Spinone Italiano may have developed behaviors not suitable for the new household. Therefore bringing a mature Spinone Italiano into the home should always be done on a trial basis.

problems in the Spinone Italiano breed that conscientious breeders strive to avoid through screening and rigid selection of breeding stock.

CANINE CEREBELLAR ATAXIA (CCA)

Research indicates that cerebellar ataxia is an inheritable disease of the cerebellum, the part of the brain that controls a dog's gait. Affected dogs have a poorly controlled or wobbly gait, and these symptoms all have been found in young dogs. Studies have confirmed that the disease is caused by a simple recessive gene. Strict controls in the selection of breeding stock are necessary in order to rid lines of the problem and to prevent the disease from being transmitted further.

HIP DYSPLASIA

Hip dysplasia is a developmental disease of the hip joint. The result is instability of the hip joint due to abnormal contours of one or both of the hip joints. Affected dogs might show tenderness in the hip, walk with a limp or swaying gait or experience difficulty when getting up after sleeping. Hip dysplasia first appears during growing stages and usually becomes progressively worse as the dog grows older. Controversy surrounds this disease regarding its genetic basis. It is now believed that, while

A good way to keep the Spinone busy is to get him wet! Although not a water dog by nature, many excel at water retrieving and enjoy a good swim.

propensity for the condition can be inherited, it is yet another condition that can be promoted by improper feeding and over-supplementation in puppies and young dogs as well as by environmental factors.

A surgical procedure to replace affected hips has been developed. All breeding stock and any dog that exhibits suspicious symptoms should be x-rayed and the problem discussed with both the breeder from whom you purchased your dog and your veterinarian.

BLOAT

Although bloat (gastric torsion) is not actually known to be an inherited problem, it does occur in deep-chested breeds such as the Spinone Italiano. Little is known about the actual cause of bloat. Many theories have been

What Is "Bloat" and How Do I Prevent it?

You likely have heard the term "bloat," which refers to gastric torsion (gastric dilatation/volvulus), a potentially fatal condition. As it is directly related to feeding and exercise practices, a brief explanation here is warranted. The term *dilatation* means that the dog's stomach is filled with air, while *volvulus* means that the stomach is twisted around on itself, blocking the entrance/exit points. Dilatation/volvulus is truly a deadly combination, although they also can occur independently of each other. An affected dog cannot digest food or pass gas, and blood cannot flow to the stomach, causing accumulation of toxins and gas along with great pain and rapidly occurring shock.

Many theories exist on what exactly causes bloat, but we do know that deep-chested breeds are more prone and that the risk doubles after seven years of age. Activities like eating a large meal, gulping water, strenuous exercise too close to mealtimes or a combination of these factors can contribute to bloat, though not every case is directly related to these more well-known causes. With that in mind, we can focus on incorporating simple daily preventives and knowing how to recognize the symptoms. In addition to the tips presented in this book, ask your vet about how to prevent and recognize bloat. An affected dog needs immediate veterinary attention, as death can result quickly. Signs include obvious restlessness/discomfort, crying in pain, drooling/excessive salivation, unproductive attempts to vomit or relieve himself, hardened abdomen, visibly bloated appearance and collapsing. Do not wait: get to the vet *right away* if you see any of these symptoms. The vet will confirm by x-ray if the stomach is bloated with air; if so, the dog must be treated *immediately*.

As varied as the causes of bloat are the tips for prevention, but some common preventive methods follow:
• Feed two or three small meals daily rather than one large one;
• Do not allow water before, after or with meals, but allow access to water at all other times;
• Never permit rapid eating or gulping of water;
• No exercise for the dog at least one hour before and two hours after meals;
• Feed high-quality food with adequate protein, adequate fiber content and not too much fat and carbohydrate;
• Explore herbal additives, enzymes or gas-reduction products (only under a vet's advice) to encourage a "friendly" environment in the dog's digestive system;
• Avoid foods and ingredients known to produce gas;
• Avoid stressful or overly excited situations for the dog, especially at mealtimes;
• Make dietary changes gradually, over a period of a few weeks;
• Do not feed dry food only;
• Although the role of genetics as a causative of bloat is not known, many breeders do not breed from previously affected dogs;
• Sometimes owners are advised to have gastroplexy (stomach stapling) performed on their dogs as a preventive measure.
Pay attention to your dog's behavior and any changes that could be symptomatic of bloat. Your dog's life depends on it!

offered but none actually proven. This often-fatal condition seems to occur frequently at night after the dog has had a large meal, has ingested a great deal of water and then exercises strenuously. Symptoms can range from a severe attack of gas to death. It can occur so suddenly and swiftly that only immediate attention from a vet experienced in dealing with the condition can save your dog's life.

Simply described, bloat causes the stomach to twist so that both ends are closed off. The food contained in the stomach ferments but gases cannot escape, thereby causing the stomach to swell, greatly pressuring the entire diaphragm and consequently leading to extreme cardiac and respiratory complications. The affected dog is in extreme pain, and death can follow very quickly unless the gas is released through surgery.

EYE PROBLEMS

The Spinone Italiano's loose skin can create a number of problems manifesting themselves in and surrounding the eyes. Entropion and ectropion in puppies and adolescents can be temporary, lasting only until maturity is reached and full size is achieved, taking up the loose skin. These conditions can persist into adulthood and may require veterinary assistance including surgery in some cases.

KEEP YOUR SPINONE ITALIANO BUSY

A bored Spinone Italiano is a chewing Spinone Italiano. Sufficient exercise helps keep that high energy level in check and is the best deterrent for chewing. In preparation for field work, the puppy can be introduced to a game bird wing. Watching this meeting awaken the innate hunting instinct that lies just below the surface of every Spinone Italiano's consciousness can be a delight for both dog and owner.

Entropion is an anatomical abnormality due to spasm and contraction of the muscles controlling the eye rims. This causes the affected eyelids to turn and roll in towards the eyeball. The resulting contact of eyelash to eyeball produces a state of semi-permanent irritation and possible permanent damage to the eyeball itself. Usually it is the lower lid that is affected but the upper lid may be affected as well. Ectropion is the scientific term for exceedingly loose lower eyelids, causing inflammation of the exposed areas of the eye and tear overflow.

INTRODUCTION TO THE STANDARD

In the earliest days of man's relationship with dogs, he began to see that those particular dogs constructed in a certain way were more successful at performing the tasks assigned to them. It then became those particular characteristics that guided man's breeding practices. The people who kept the dogs that were serving them best gathered to make comparisons and seek out stock to improve their own dogs. The more successful keepers were asked to observe the dogs at work and evaluate them.

With industrialization, little villages grew into large cities and towns, and the citizenry moved into urban dwellings. Fewer and fewer dogs were given the opportunity to perform in the capacity for which their breeds were created. To avoid the respective breeds' losing their ability to perform, dog fanciers began to select their stock on the basis of the conformation that they determined would produce the most successful workers. The guidelines, or "standards," became theoretical rather than practical. It should be noted here that these descriptions were the forerunners of what are known as "breed standards" today and that they were written by knowledgeable individuals in the breed for their peers. The descriptions were used primarily as checklists or "blueprints" to breed by, and they served as reminders so that important points of conformation would not be lost.

In many cases, the accent that had previously been on function was now placed on form. It should be easy to see, once form was the keynote, how breeds whose only purpose was to be esthetically pleasing would gain an equal place of respect alongside their working relatives. It should be understood, however, that not all fanciers neglected the original purpose of their breeds. For example, in Italy, devotees of the Spinone Italiano jealously have guarded the breed's hunting ability through the centuries and have been adamant in maintaining the characteristics that enable their breed to excel in this capacity.

Today's Spinone Italiano standard describes the ideal hunting dog. It is based upon the original standard drafted in Italy that was written by individuals versed in the breed's type and ability in the field. It includes a description of ideal structure, temperament, coat, color and gait (the manner in which the breed moves). All of these descriptions are based upon what constitutes an efficient hunter and reliable companion.

As stated, breed standards are used by breeders to assist them in breeding toward their goal of perfection. While no dog is absolutely perfect, the dogs that adhere most closely to the ideal are what breeders will determine to be show or breeding stock, and the dogs that deviate to any great extent are considered companion or pet stock. The standard is also used by dog show judges to compare actual dogs to the ideal. The dog adhering most closely to this ideal is the winner of its class, and so on down the line.

AMERICAN KENNEL CLUB STANDARD FOR THE SPINONE ITALIANO

General Appearance
Muscular dog with powerful bone. Vigorous and robust, his purpose as hardworking gun dog is evident. Naturally sociable, the docile and patient Spinone is resistant to fatigue and is an experienced hunter on any terrain. His hard textured coat is weather resistant. His wiry, dense coat and thick skin enable the Spinone to negotiate underbrush and endure cold water that would severely punish any dog not so naturally armored. He has a remarkable tendency for an extended and fast trotting gait. The Spinone is an excellent retriever by nature.

Size, Proportion, Substance
Height: The height at the withers is 23 to 27 inches for males and 22 to 25 inches for females. *Weight:* In direct proportion to size and structure of dog. *Proportion*: His build tends to fit into a square. The length of the body, measured from sternum to point of buttocks, is approximately equal to the height at the withers with tolerance of no more than 1 inch in length compared to height. *Substance*: The Spinone is a solidly built dog, robust with powerful bone.

Head
Long. The profile of the Spinone is unique to this breed. Expression is of paramount importance to the breed. It should denote intelligence and gentleness. Skull of oval shape,

An ideal Spinone Italiano in profile, showing desired structure, substance and proportion.

An artist's sketch of the correct Spinone Italiano head.

brown) in color, darker eyes with darker colored dogs, lighter eyes with lighter colored dogs. Large, well opened, set well apart, the eye is almost round, the lids closely fitting the eye, to protect the eye from gathering debris while the dog is hunting, loose eye lids must be faulted. Which is neither protruding nor deep set. Eye rim clearly visible, color will vary with coat color from flesh colored to brown. Disqualification: Walleye. *Nose:* Bulbous and spongy in appearance with upper edge rounded. Nostrils are large and well opened. In profile, the nose protrudes past the forward line of the lips. (Pigment is flesh colored in white dogs, darker in white and orange dogs, brown in brown or brown roan dogs.) Disqualification: Any pigment other than described or incomplete pigment of the nose is to be disqualified. *Teeth*: Jaw is powerful. Teeth are positioned in a scissors or level bite. Disqualification: Overshot or undershot bite. *Ears:* Practically triangular shape. Set on a level just below the eye, carried low, with little erectile power. The leather is fine, covered with short, thick hair mixed with a longer sparser hair, which becomes thicker along edges. Length, if measured along the head would extend to tip of nose and no more than 1 inch beyond the tip. The forward edge is adherent to the cheek, not folded, but turned outward; the tip of the ear is slightly rounded.

with sides gently sloping. With occipital protuberance well developed, medial-frontal furrow is very pronounced. *Muzzle:* Square when viewed from the front. Muzzle length is equal to that of backskull. The planes of the skull and muzzle are diverging, downfaced. Its width measured at its midpoint is a third of its length. Stop is barely perceptible. Bridge of the muzzle is preferably slightly Roman, however, straight is not to be faulted. *Lips* fitting tightly to the jawline. Convergence of planes of the skull and muzzle or a dish-faced muzzle is to be faulted so severely as to eliminate from further competition. *Eyes:* Must have a soft sweet expression. Ochre (yellowish

Neck, Topline, Body

Neck: Strong, thick, and muscular. Clearly defined from the nape, blending in to the shoulders in a harmonious line. The throat is moderate in skin with a double dewlap. *Chest:* Broad, deep, well muscled and well rounded; extending at least to the elbow. The ribs are well sprung. The distance from ground to the elbow is equal to half the height at the withers. *Back:* The topline consists of two segments. The first slopes slightly downward in a nearly straight line from the withers to the 11th thoracic vertebrae, approximately 6 inches behind the withers. The second rises gradually and continues into a solid and well-arched loin. The underline is solid and should have minimal tuck up. *Croup:* Well muscled, long. The hipbones fall away from the spinal column at an angle of about 30 degrees, producing a lightly rounded, well filled-out croup. *Tail:* Follows the line of the croup, thick at the base, carried horizontally or down; flicking from side to side while moving is preferred. The tail should lack fringes. It is docked to a length of 5.5 to 8 inches. Tail habitually carried above the level of the back or straight up when working is to be penalized.

Forequarters

Shoulders: Powerful and long, withers not too prominent; forming an angle with the upper arm of approximately angle 105. With well-developed muscles, the points of the shoulder blades are not close together. The ideal distance between the shoulder blades is approximately two inches or more. Angulation of shoulder is in balance with angulation in the rear. *Forelegs:* The forelegs are straight when viewed from the front angle with strong bone and well-developed muscles; elbows set under the withers and close to the body. Pasterns are long, lean and flexible following the vertical line of the forearm. In profile, they are slightly slanted. *Feet:* Large compact, rounded with well-arched toes, which are close together, covered with short, dense hair, including between the toes. Pads are lean and hard with strong nails curving toward the ground, well pigmented, but never black. Dewclaws may be removed.

Hindquarters

Thighs are strong and well muscled, stifles show good function angulation, lower thigh to be well developed and muscled with good

Correct structure is of utmost importance, especially in a breed whose construction enables it to perform its intended duty. In the show ring, the judge feels to make sure that correct bone structure is present.

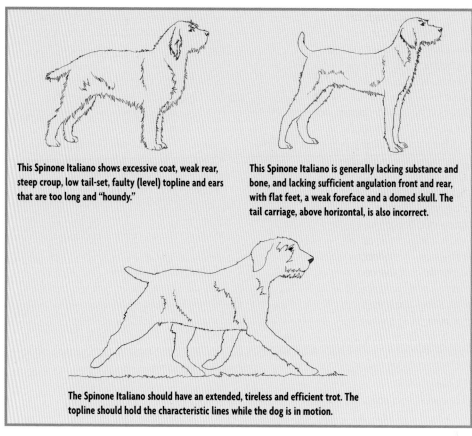

This Spinone Italiano shows excessive coat, weak rear, steep croup, low tail-set, faulty (level) topline and ears that are too long and "houndy."

This Spinone Italiano is generally lacking substance and bone, and lacking sufficient angulation front and rear, with flat feet, a weak foreface and a domed skull. The tail carriage, above horizontal, is also incorrect.

The Spinone Italiano should have an extended, tireless and efficient trot. The topline should hold the characteristic lines while the dog is in motion.

breadth. The hock, with proportion of one-third the distance from the hip joint to foot being ideal, is strong, lean and perpendicular to the ground. Fault: Cowhocks. *Feet:* Slightly more oval than the forefoot with the same characteristics. Dewclaws may be removed.

Skin

The skin must be very thick, closely fitting the body. The skin is thinner on the head, throat, groin, under the legs and in the folds of the elbows is

soft to the touch. Pigmentation is dependent upon the color or markings of the coat. Disqualification: Any black pigmentation.

Coat

A Spinone must have a correct coat to be of correct type. The ideal coat length is 1.5 to 2.5 inches on the body, with a tolerance of one-half inch over or under the ideal length. Head, ears, muzzle and front sides of legs and feet are covered by shorter hair. The hair on the backsides of the legs forms a rough brush, but there are never any fringes. The eyes and lips are framed by stiff hair forming eyebrows, mustache and tufted beard, which combine to save fore face from laceration by briar and bush. The coat is dense, stiff and flat or slightly crimped, but not curly, with an absence of undercoat. The Spinone is exhibited in a natural state. The appearance of the Spinone may not be altered. The dog must present the natural appearance of a functional field dog. Dogs with a long, soft or silky coat, the presence of undercoat, or any deviation of the coat as defined in this as well as excessive grooming, i.e., scissoring, clipping or setting of pattern shall be severely penalized as to eliminate them from further competition.

Color
The accepted colors are: Solid white, white and orange; orange roan with or without orange markings; white with brown markings, brown roan with or without brown markings. The most desired color of brown is chestnut brown, "monks habit," however, varying colors of brown are acceptable. Disqualification: Any black in the coat, tan, tri-color, in any combination, or any color other than accepted colors.

Gait
The Spinone is first and foremost a functional working gun dog. Its purpose as a versatile hunting dog must be given the utmost consideration. Easy and loose trot geared for endurance. Maximum ground is covered with least amount of effort, which his purpose as a versatile working gun dog demands. Profile of the topline kept throughout the trotting gait, light body roll in mature bitches is characteristic of the breed. While hunting, an extended fast trot with intermittent paces of a gallop allows the Spinone to cover ground quickly and thoroughly. Any characteristics that interfere with the accomplishment of the function of the Spinone shall be considered as a serious fault.

Faults
Any departure from the foregoing points constitutes a fault which when judging must be penalized according to its seriousness and extension.

Disqualification
- Wall eye.
- Any pigment other than described or incomplete pigment of the nose.
- Overshot or undershot bite.
- Any black pigmentation.
- Any black in the coat; tan, tri-color markings in any combination or any color other than accepted colors.

Approved: February 11, 2000
Effective: September 28, 2000

SPINONE ITALIANO

dogs shown in conformation competition, obedience, etc? If the person with whom you are talking breeds Spinoni only to sell pet puppies, go somewhere else for your dog!

FINDING A QUALIFIED BREEDER

Before you begin your puppy search, ask for references from the Spinone Club of America, your veterinarian and perhaps other breeders to refer you to someone they believe is reputable. Responsible breeders usually raise only one or two breeds of dog. Avoid any breeder who has several different breeds or has several litters at the same time. Dedicated breeders are usually involved with a breed or other dog club. Many participate in some sport or activity related to their breed. Just as you want to be assured of the breeder's qualifications, the breeder wants to be assured that you will make a worthy owner. Expect the breeder to interview you, asking questions about your goals for the pup, your experience with dogs and what kind of home you will provide.

While it is hard to predict show quality in young pups, quality pups come from quality breeding. Breeders have knowledge of their own lines and should have an idea of how their pups will develop.

HOW TO SELECT A SPINONE BREEDER AND PUPPY

Your Spinone should only be purchased from a breeder who has earned a reputation for consistently producing dogs that are mentally and physically sound. The only way a breeder can earn this reputation is through selective breeding aimed at eliminating genetic weaknesses.

The first question a prospective owner should ask a Spinone breeder is, "What do you do with your dogs?" Does he hunt his dogs or compete in field trials? Are the

Cleanliness in both the dogs and the areas in which the dogs are kept is a bottom-line requirement, so take note of this when you visit the facility. This is the first clue that tells you how much the breeder cares about the dogs he owns.

The Spinone puppy you buy should be a happy and bouncy extrovert. However, you need not necessarily select the leader of the little pack. The extremely bold and extroverted pup will undoubtedly demand a lot more exercise and attention to keep him wound down than will his calmer, content littermates. This does not mean you should select a shy, shrinking-violet puppy. This, of course, is not typical of correct Spinone attitude.

Healthy Spinone puppies are strong and firm to the touch, never bony or, on the other hand, obese and bloated. Coats will be lustrous with no sign of dry or flaky skin. The inside of the puppy's ears should be pink and clean. Dark discharge or a bad odor could indicate ear mites, a sure sign of poor maintenance. The healthy Spinone puppy's breath smells sweet. The teeth are clean and white, and there should never be any malformation of the mouth or jaw. The puppy's eyes should be

You can learn quite a bit about the puppies' future temperaments by observing them at play with their parents and littermates.

MALE OR FEMALE?

Males of most dog breeds tend to be larger than their female counterparts and take longer to mature. Males also can be more dominant and territorial, especially if they are sexually intact. Neutering before one year of age can help minimize those tendencies. Females of most breeds are often less rambunctious and easier to handle. However, individual personalities vary, so the differences are often due more to temperament than to the sex of the animal.

clear and bright. Eyes that appear runny and irritated indicate serious problems. There should be no sign of discharge from the nose nor should it ever be crusted or runny. Coughing and diarrhea are danger signals, as are any eruptions on the skin. The breeder should show you hereditary health clearances on the pups' parents and health records on the puppies.

The healthy Spinone puppy's front legs should be straight as little posts. Even at an early age, a Spinone puppy's legs appear long in proportion and give the youngster a somewhat awkward gangly look. Yet movement is true, and there should be no hint of lameness or difficulty when moving.

If you are considering a show career for your puppy, you should be aware that the most any breeder can offer is an opinion on the "show potential" of a particular puppy. Any predictions that breeders make about a puppy's future should be based upon their experience with past litters that have produced winning show dogs. It is obvious that the more successful a breeder has been in producing winning Spinoni over the years, the broader his or her base of comparison will be. Give serious consideration to both what the standard says a show-type Spinone must look like and to the breeder's recommendations.

A COMMITTED NEW OWNER

By now you should understand what makes the Spinone a most unique and special dog, one that may fit nicely into your family and lifestyle. If you have researched breeders, you should be able to recognize a knowledgeable and responsible Spinone breeder who cares not only about his pups but also about what kind of owner you will be. If you have completed the final step in your new journey, you have found a litter, or possibly two, of quality Spinone pups.

A visit with the puppies and their breeder should be an education in itself. Breed research, breeder selection and puppy visitation are very important aspects of finding the puppy of your dreams. Beyond that, these things also lay the foundation for a successful future with your pup. Puppy personalities within each litter vary, from the shy and easygoing puppy to the one who is dominant and assertive, with most pups falling somewhere in between. By spending time with the puppies you will be able to recognize certain behaviors and what these behaviors indicate about each pup's temperament. Which type of pup will complement your family dynamics is best determined by observing the puppies in action within their "pack." Your breeder's expertise and recommendations are also valuable. Although you may fall in love with a bold and brassy male, the breeder may suggest that another pup would be best for

Welcoming your new Spinone pup home is an exciting and joyful occasion!

The selection of a Spinone Italiano represents a big commitment from a new owner. This active breed requires an owner who can be "on call" from the early days of house-training through the many school days that follow.

you. The breeder's experience in rearing Spinone pups and matching their temperaments with appropriate humans offers the best assurance that your pup will meet your needs and expectations. The type of puppy that you select is just as important as your decision that the Spinone is the breed for you.

The decision to live with a Spinone is a serious commitment and not one to be taken lightly. This puppy is a living sentient being that will be dependent on you for basic survival for his entire life. Beyond the basics of survival—food, water, shelter and protection—he needs much, much more. The new pup needs love, nurturing and a proper canine education to mold him into a responsible, well-behaved canine citizen. Your Spinone's health and good manners will need consistent monitoring and regular "tune-ups," so your job as a responsible dog owner will be ongoing throughout every stage of his life. If you are not prepared to accept these responsibilities and commit to them for the next decade, likely longer, then you are not prepared to own a dog of any breed.

Select a sturdy crate for your Spinone, in a size that will accommodate him when fully grown.

Although the responsibilities of owning a dog may at times tax your patience, the joy of living with your Spinone far outweighs the workload, and a well-mannered adult dog is worth your time and effort. Before your very eyes, your new charge will grow up to be your most loyal friend, devoted to you unconditionally.

YOUR SPINONE ITALIANO SHOPPING LIST

Just as expectant parents prepare a nursery for their baby, so should you ready your home for the arrival of your Spinone pup. If you have the necessary puppy supplies purchased and in place before he comes home, it will ease the puppy's transition from the warmth and familiarity of his mom and littermates to the brand-new environment of his new home and human family. You will be too busy to stock up and prepare your house after your pup comes home, that's for sure! Imagine how a pup must feel upon being transported to a strange new place. It's up to you to comfort him and to let your little pup know that he is going to be happy with you.

FOOD AND WATER BOWLS
Your puppy will need separate bowls for his food and water. Stainless steel pans are generally preferred over plastic bowls

since they sterilize better and pups are less inclined to chew on the metal. Heavy-duty ceramic bowls are popular, but consider how often you will have to pick up those heavy bowls. Buy adult-sized pans, as your puppy will grow into them quickly.

THE DOG CRATE

If you think that crates are tools of punishment and confinement for when a dog has misbehaved, think again. Most breeders and almost all trainers recommend a crate as the preferred house-training aid as well as for all-around puppy training and safety. Because dogs are natural den creatures that prefer cave-like environments, the benefits of crate use are many. The crate provides the puppy with his very own "safe house," a cozy place to sleep, take a break or seek comfort with a favorite toy; a travel aid to house your dog when on the road, at motels or at the vet's office; a training aid to help teach your puppy proper toileting habits; a place of solitude when non-dog people happen to drop by and don't want a lively puppy—or even a well-behaved adult dog—saying hello or begging for attention.

Crates come in several types, although the wire crate and the fiberglass airline-type crate are the most popular. Both are safe and your puppy will adjust to either one, so the choice is up to you. The wire crates offer better visibility for the pup as well as better ventilation. Many of the wire crates easily collapse into suitcase-size carriers. The fiberglass crates, similar to those used by the airlines for animal transport, are sturdier and more

GETTING ACQUAINTED

When visiting a litter, ask the breeder for suggestions on how best to interact with the puppies. If possible, get right into the middle of the pack and sit down with them. Observe which pups climb into your lap and which ones shy away. Toss a toy for them to chase and bring back to you. It's easy to fall in love with the puppy who picks you, but keep your future objectives in mind before you make your final decision.

den-like. However, the fiberglass crates do not collapse and are less ventilated than a wire crate; this can be problematic in hot weather. Some of the newer crates are made of heavy plastic mesh; they are very lightweight and fold up into slim-line suitcases. However, a mesh crate might not be suitable for a pup with manic chewing habits.

Don't bother with a puppy-sized crate. Although your Spinone will be a wee fellow when you bring him home, he will grow up in the blink of an eye and your puppy crate will be useless. Purchase a crate that will accommodate an adult Spinone. He will stand about 23–27 inches at the shoulder when full grown, so a large-sized crate will be needed. Keep in mind that he will need to be able to fully stand, lie down and turn around comfortably in his crate.

Spinone puppies grow like weeds. This young puppy is nearly too heavy to carry (and has already grown out of his puppy crate).

NEW RELEASES
Most breeders release their puppies between eight and ten weeks of age. A breeder who allows puppies to leave the litter at five or six weeks of age may be more concerned with profit than with the puppies' welfare. However, some breeders of show or working breeds may hold one or more top-quality puppies longer, occasionally until three or four months of age, in order to evaluate the puppies' career or show potential and decide which one(s) they will keep for themselves.

BEDDING AND CRATE PADS
Your puppy will enjoy some type of soft bedding in his "room" (the crate), something he can snuggle into to feel cozy and secure. Old towels or blankets are good choices for a young pup, since he may (and probably will) have a toileting accident or two in the crate or decide to chew on the bedding material. Once he is fully trained and out of the early chewing stage, you can replace the puppy bedding with a permanent crate pad if you prefer. Crate pads and other dog beds run the gamut from inexpensive to high-end doggie-designer styles, but don't splurge on the good stuff until you are sure that your puppy is reliable and won't tear it up or make a mess on it.

PUPPY TOYS

Just as infants and older children require objects to stimulate their minds and bodies, puppies need toys to entertain their curious brains, wiggly paws and achy teeth. A fun array of safe doggie toys will help satisfy your puppy's chewing instincts and distract him from gnawing on the leg of your antique chair or your new leather sofa. Most puppy toys are cute and look as if they would be a lot of fun, but not all are necessarily safe or good for your puppy, so use caution when you go puppy-toy shopping.

Although Spinoni are not known to be voracious chewers like many other dogs, they still love to chew. The best "chewci-fiers" are nylon and hard rubber bones which are safe to gnaw on and come in sizes appropriate for all age groups and breeds. Be especially careful of natural bones, which can splinter or develop dangerous sharp edges; pups can easily swallow or choke on those bone splinters. Veterinarians often tell of surgical nightmares involving bits of splintered bone because in addition to the danger of choking, the sharp pieces can damage the intestinal tract.

Similarly, rawhide chews, while a favorite of most dogs and puppies, can be equally dangerous. Pieces of rawhide are easily swallowed after they get

TOYS 'R SAFE

The vast array of tantalizing puppy toys is staggering. Stroll through any pet shop or pet-supply outlet and you will see that the choices can be overwhelming. However, not all dog toys are safe or sensible. Most very young puppies enjoy soft woolly toys that they can snuggle with and carry around. (You know they have outgrown them when they shred them up!) Avoid toys that have buttons, tabs or other enhancements that can be chewed off and swallowed. Soft toys that squeak are fun, but make sure your puppy does not disembowel the toy and remove (and swallow) the squeaker. Toys that rattle or make noise can excite a puppy, but they present the same danger as the squeaky kind and so require supervision. Hard rubber toys that bounce can also entertain a pup, but make sure that the toy is too big for your pup to swallow.

These two Spinone pups are sniffing their first rope toy. Be careful, as the strings can be dangerous if ingested by a pup.

soft and gummy from chewing, and dogs have been known to choke on large pieces of ingested rawhide. Rawhide chews should be offered only when you can supervise the puppy.

Soft woolly toys are special puppy favorites. They come in a wide variety of cute shapes and sizes; some look like little stuffed animals. Puppies love to shake them up and toss them about, or simply carry them around. Be careful of fuzzy toys that have button eyes or noses that your pup could chew off and swallow, and make sure that he does not disembowel a squeaky toy to remove the squeaker! Braided rope toys are similar in that they are fun to chew and toss around, but they shred easily and the strings are easy to swallow. The strings are not digestible and, if the puppy doesn't pass them in his stool, he could end up at the vet's office. As with rawhides, your puppy should be closely monitored with rope toys.

If you believe that your pup has ingested a piece of one of his toys, check his stools for the next couple of days to see if he passes the item when he defecates. At the same time, also watch for signs of intestinal distress. A call to your veterinarian might be in order to get his advice and be on the safe side.

An all-time favorite toy for puppies (young and old!) is the empty gallon milk jug. Hard plastic juice containers—46 ounces or more—are also excellent. Such containers make lots of noise when they are batted about, and puppies go crazy with delight as they play with them. However, they don't often last very long, so be sure to remove

COST OF OWNERSHIP

The purchase price of your puppy is merely the first expense in the typical dog budget. Quality dog food, veterinary care (sickness and health maintenance), dog supplies and grooming costs will add up to big bucks every year. Can you adequately afford to support a canine addition to the family?

COLLARING OUR CANINES

The standard flat collar with a buckle or a snap, in leather, nylon or cotton, is widely regarded as the everyday all-purpose collar. If the collar fits correctly, you should be able to fit two fingers between the collar and the dog's neck.

Leather Buckle Collars

Limited-Slip Collar

The martingale, Greyhound or limited-slip collar is preferred by many dog owners and trainers. It is fixed with an extra loop that tightens when pressure is applied to the leash. The martingale collar gets tighter but does not "choke" the dog. The limited-slip collar should only be used for walking and training, not for free play or interaction with another dog. These types of collar should never be left on the dog, as the extra loop can lead to accidents.

Choke collars, usually made of stainless steel, are made for training purposes but are not recommended for small dogs or heavily coated breeds. The chains can injure small dogs or damage long/abundant coats. Thin nylon choke leads are commonly used on show dogs while in the ring, though they are not practical for everyday use.

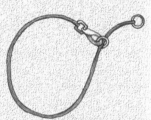

Snap-Bolt Choke Collar

The harness, with two or three straps that attach over the dog's shoulders and around his torso, is a humane and safe alternative to the conventional collar. By and large, a well-made harness is virtually escape-proof. Harnesses are available in nylon and mesh and can be outfitted on most dogs with chest girths ranging from 10 to 30 inches.

Harness

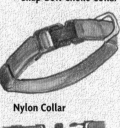

Nylon Collar

Quick-Click Closure

Snake Chain

Chrome Steel

Fur-Saver

Choke Chain Collars

A head collar, composed of a nylon strap that goes around the dog's muzzle and a second strap that wraps around his neck, offers the owner better control over his dog. This device is recommended for problem-solving with dogs (including jumping up, pulling and aggressive behaviors), but must be used with care.

A training halter, including a flat collar and two straps, made of nylon and webbing, is designed for walking. There are several on the market; some are more difficult to put on the dog than others. The halter harness, with two small slip rings at each end, is recommended for ease of use.

Leash Life

Dogs love leashes! Believe it or not, most dogs dance for joy every time their owners pick up their leashes. The leash means that the dog is going for a walk—and there are few things more exciting than that! Here are some of the kinds of leashes that are commercially available.

Nylon Leash

Leather Leash

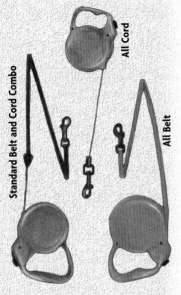

Standard Belt and Cord Combo

All Cord

All Belt

Retractable Leashes

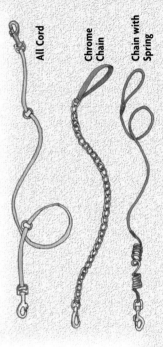

All Cord

Chrome Chain

Chain with Spring

Traditional Leash: Made of cotton, nylon or leather, these leashes are usually about 6 feet in length. A quality-made leather leash is softer on the hands than a nylon one. Durable woven cotton is a popular option. Lengths can vary up to about 48 feet, designed for different uses.

Chain Leash: Usually a metal chain leash with a plastic handle. This is not the best choice for most breeds, as it is heavier than other leashes and difficult to manage.

Retractable Leash: A long nylon cord is housed in a plastic device for extending and retracting. This leash, also known as a flexible leash, is ideal for taking trained dogs for long walks in open areas, although it is not always suitable for large, powerful breeds. Different lengths and sizes are available, so check that you purchase one appropriate for your dog's weight.

Elastic Leash: A nylon leash with an elastic extension. This is useful for well-trained dogs, especially in conjunction with a head halter.

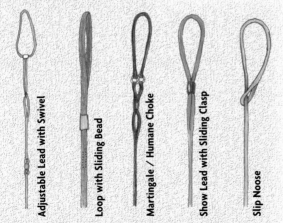

Adjustable Lead with Swivel

Loop with Sliding Bead

Martingale / Humane Choke

Show Lead with Sliding Clasp

Slip Noose

A Variety of Collar-Leash-in-One Products

Avoid leashes that are completely elastic, as they afford minimal control to the handler.

Adjustable Leash: This has two snaps, one on each end, and several metal rings. It is handy if you need to tether your dog temporarily, but is never to be used with a choke collar.

Tab Leash: A short leash (4 to 6 inches long) that attaches to your dog's collar. This device serves like a handle, in case you have to grab your dog while he's exercising off lead. It's ideal for "half-trained" dogs or dogs that listen only half of the time.

Slip Leash: Essentially a leash with a collar built in, similar to what a dog-show handler uses to show a dog. This British-style collar has a ring on the end so that you can form a slip collar. Useful if you have to catch your own runaway dog or a stray.

A Spinone pup using those "puppy-dog eyes" to see if he can entice his owner into playing a game of fetch with his favorite toy.

and replace them when they get chewed up.

A word of caution about homemade toys: be careful with your choices of non-traditional play objects. Never use old shoes or socks, since a puppy cannot distinguish between the old ones on which he's allowed to chew and the new ones in your closet that are strictly off limits. That principle applies to anything that resembles something that you don't want your puppy to chew.

COLLARS

A lightweight nylon collar is the best choice for a very young pup. Quick-click collars are easy to put on and remove, and they can be adjusted as the puppy grows. Introduce him to his collar as soon as he comes home to get him accustomed to wearing it.

He'll get used to it quickly and won't mind a bit. Make sure that it is snug enough that it won't slip off, yet loose enough to be comfortable for the pup. You should be able to slip two fingers between the collar and his neck. Check the collar often, as puppies grow in spurts, and his collar can become too tight almost overnight. Choke collars are for training purposes only and should never be used on a puppy. Many trainers recommend head collars for training the adult dog instead, and these humane devices are worth exploring, especially if your dog proves more difficult to train.

LEASHES

A 6-foot nylon lead is an excellent choice for a young puppy. It is lightweight and not as tempting to

A Dog-Safe Home

The dog-safety police are taking you on a house tour. Let's go room by room and see how safe your own home is for your new pup. The following items are doggie dangers, so either they must be removed or the dog should be monitored or not allowed access to these areas.

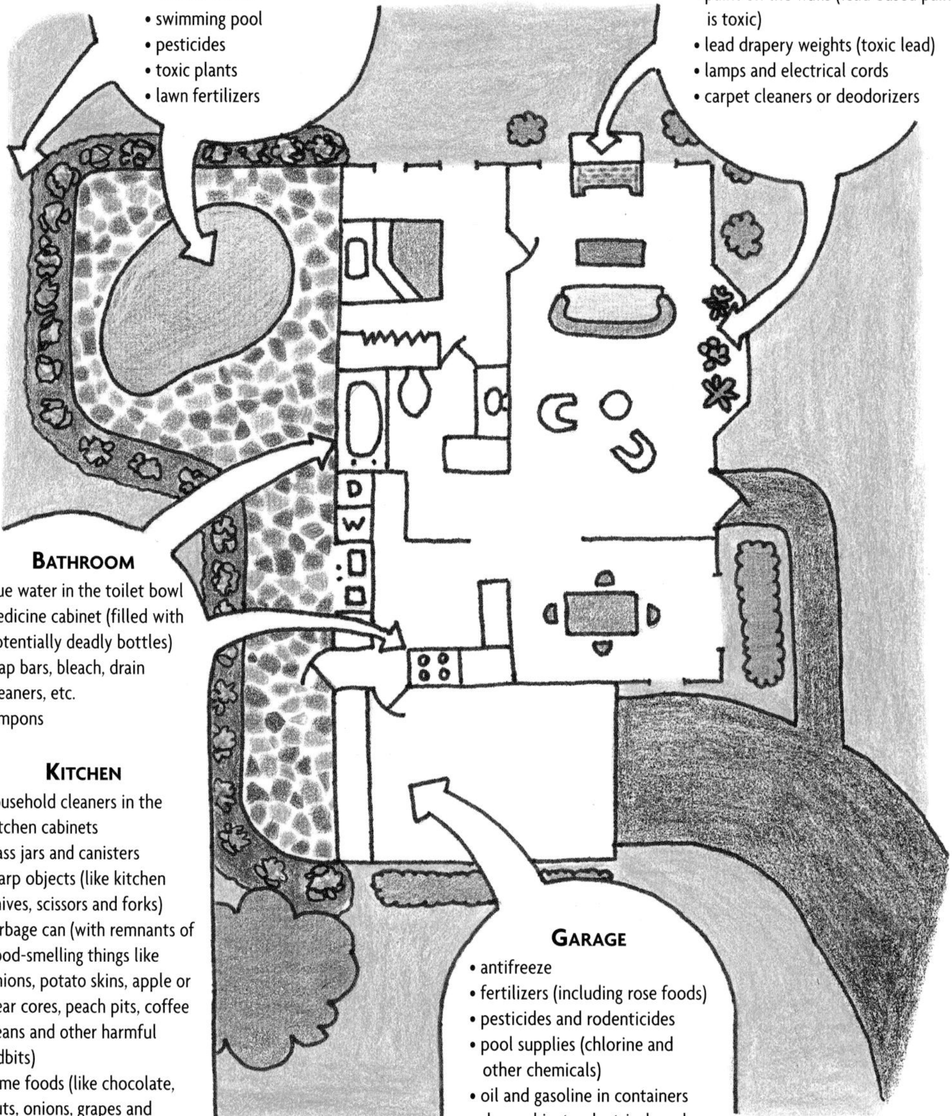

Living Room

- house plants (some varieties are poisonous)
- fireplace or wood-burning stove
- paint on the walls (lead-based paint is toxic)
- lead drapery weights (toxic lead)
- lamps and electrical cords
- carpet cleaners or deodorizers

Outdoors

- swimming pool
- pesticides
- toxic plants
- lawn fertilizers

Bathroom

- blue water in the toilet bowl
- medicine cabinet (filled with potentially deadly bottles)
- soap bars, bleach, drain cleaners, etc.
- tampons

Kitchen

- household cleaners in the kitchen cabinets
- glass jars and canisters
- sharp objects (like kitchen knives, scissors and forks)
- garbage can (with remnants of good-smelling things like onions, potato skins, apple or pear cores, peach pits, coffee beans and other harmful tidbits)
- some foods (like chocolate, nuts, onions, grapes and raisins) are toxic to dogs

Garage

- antifreeze
- fertilizers (including rose foods)
- pesticides and rodenticides
- pool supplies (chlorine and other chemicals)
- oil and gasoline in containers
- sharp objects, electrical cords and power tools

chew as a leather lead. You can switch to a 6-foot leather lead after your pup has grown and is used to walking politely on a lead. For initial puppy walks and house-training purposes, you should invest in a shorter lead so that you have more control over the puppy. At first you don't want him wandering too far away from you, and when taking him out for toileting you will want to keep him in the specific area chosen for his potty spot.

Once the puppy is heel-trained with a traditional leash, you can consider purchasing a retractable lead. A retractable lead is excellent for walking adult dogs that are already leash-wise. This type of lead allows the dog to roam farther away from you and

The profuse, wiry coat of the Spinone can make the dog's collar tight and uncomfortable. Do not place the collar on too tightly, and check it regularly.

Don't forget that your Spinone puppy is a hunting dog who specializes in birds. Owners who intend to work their dogs in the field introduce young puppies to game to give them the scent and sense of the hunt.

THE FIRST FAMILY MEETING

Your puppy's first day at home should be quiet and uneventful. Despite his wagging tail, he is still wondering where his mom and siblings are! Let him make friends with other members of the family on his own terms; don't overwhelm him. You have a lifetime ahead to get to know each other!

Your new Spinone will be part of the family in no time!

home. There are countless hazards in the owner's personal living environment that a pup can sniff, chew, swallow or destroy. Many are obvious; others are not. Do a thorough advance house check to remove or rearrange those things that could hurt your puppy, keeping any potentially dangerous items out of areas to which he will have access.

Electrical cords are especially dangerous, since puppies view them as irresistible chew toys. Unplug and remove all exposed cords or fasten them beneath baseboards where the puppy cannot reach them. Veterinarians and firefighters can tell you horror stories about electrical burns and house fires that resulted from puppy-chewed electrical cords. Consider this a most serious precaution for your puppy and the rest of your family.

Scout your home for tiny

explore a wider area when out walking and also retracts when you need to keep him close to you. Purchase one appropriate for your Spinone's adult weight.

HOME SAFETY FOR YOUR SPINONE PUPPY

The importance of puppy-proofing cannot be overstated. In addition to making your house comfortable for your Spinone's arrival, you also must make sure that your house is safe for your puppy before you bring him

objects that might be seen at a pup's eye level. Keep medication bottles and cleaning supplies well out of reach, and do the same with waste baskets and other trash containers. It goes without saying that you should not use rodent poison or other toxic chemicals in any puppy area and that you must keep such containers safely locked up. You will be amazed at how many places a curious puppy can discover!

Once your house has cleared inspection, check your yard. A sturdy fence, well embedded into the ground, will give your dog a safe place to play and potty. Although Spinoni are not known to be climbers or fence jumpers, they are very athletic dogs, so a 6-foot-high fence is necessary to contain an agile youngster or adult. Check the fence often for necessary repairs. If there is a weak link or space to squeeze through, you can be sure a determined Spinone will discover it.

The garage and shed can be hazardous places for a pup, as things like fertilizers, chemicals and tools are usually kept there. It's best to keep these areas off limits to the pup. Antifreeze is especially dangerous to dogs, as they find the taste appealing and it takes only a few licks from the driveway to kill a dog, puppy or adult, small breed or large.

TOXIC PLANTS

Plants are natural puppy magnets, but many can be harmful, even fatal, if ingested by a puppy or adult dog. Scout your yard and home interior and remove any plants, bushes or flowers that could be even mildly dangerous. It could save your puppy's life. You can obtain a complete list of toxic plants from your veterinarian, at the public library or by looking online.

VISITING THE VETERINARIAN

A good veterinarian is your Spinone puppy's best health-insurance policy. If you do not already have a vet, ask friends and experienced dog people in your area for recommendations so that you can select a vet before you bring your Spinone puppy home. Also arrange for your puppy's first veterinary examination beforehand, since many vets may have two- and three-week waiting periods and your puppy should visit the vet within a day or so of coming home.

It's important to make sure your puppy's first visit to the vet is a pleasant and positive one. The vet should take great care to befriend the pup and handle him gently to make their first meeting a positive experience. The vet will give the pup a thorough physical examination and set up a schedule for vaccinations and other necessary wellness visits. Be sure to show your vet any health and inoculation records, which you should have received from your breeder. Your vet is a great source of canine health information, so be sure to ask questions and take notes. Creating a health

THE CRITICAL SOCIALIZATION PERIOD

Canine research has shown that a puppy's 8th through 20th week is the most critical learning period of his life. This is when the puppy "learns to learn," a time when he needs positive experiences to build confidence and stability. Puppies who are not exposed to different people and situations outside the home during this period can grow up to be fearful and sometimes aggressive. This is also the best time for puppy lessons, since he has not yet acquired any bad habits that could undermine his ability to learn.

journal for your puppy will make a handy reference for his wellness and any future health problems that may arise.

MEETING THE FAMILY

Your Spinone's homecoming is an exciting time for all members of the family, and it's only natural that everyone will be eager to meet him, pet him and play with him. However, for the puppy's sake, it's best to make these initial family meetings as uneventful as possible so that the pup is not over-whelmed with too much too soon. Remember, he has just left his dam and his littermates and is away from the breeder's home for the first time. Despite his fuzzy wagging tail, he is still apprehensive and wondering where he is and who all these strange humans are. It's best to let him explore on his own and meet the family members as he feels comfortable. Let him investigate all the new smells, sights and sounds at his own pace. Children should be especially careful to not get overly excited, use loud voices or hug the pup too tightly. Be calm, gentle and affectionate, and be ready to comfort him if he appears frightened or uneasy.

Be sure to show your puppy his new crate during this first day home. Toss a treat or two inside the crate; if he associates the crate with food, he will associate the crate with good things. If he is

comfortable with the crate, you can offer him his first meal inside it. Leave the door ajar so he can wander in and out as he chooses.

TEETHING TIME

All puppies chew. It's normal canine behavior. Chewing just plain feels good to a puppy, especially during the three- to five-month-old teething period when the adult teeth are breaking through the gums. Rather than attempting to eliminate such a strong natural chewing instinct, you will be more successful if you redirect it and teach your puppy what he may or may not chew. Correct inappropriate chewing with a sharp "No!" and offer him a chew toy, praising him when he takes it. Don't become discouraged. Chewing usually decreases after the adult teeth have come in.

MEET AND MINGLE

Puppies need to meet people and see the world if they are to grow up confident and unafraid. Take your puppy with you on everyday outings and errands. On-lead walks around the neighborhood and to the park offer the pup good exposure to the goings-on of his new human world. Avoid areas frequented by other dogs until your puppy has had his full round of puppy shots; ask your vet when your pup will be properly protected. Arrange for your puppy to meet new people of all ages every week.

FIRST NIGHT IN HIS NEW HOME

So much has happened in your Spinone puppy's first day away from the breeder. He's had his first car ride to his new home. He's met his new human family and perhaps the other family pets. He has explored his new house and yard, at least those places where he is allowed to be during his first weeks at home. He may have visited his new veterinarian. He has eaten his first meal or two away from his dam and littermates. Surely that's enough to tire out an eight-week-old Spinone pup...or so you hope!

It's bedtime. During the day, the pup investigated his crate, which is his new den and sleeping space, so it is not entirely strange to him. Line the crate with a soft towel or blanket that he can snuggle into and gently place him into the crate for the night. Some breeders send home a piece of bedding from where the pup slept with his littermates, and those familiar scents are a great comfort for the puppy on his first night without his siblings.

He will probably whine or cry. The puppy is objecting to the confinement and the fact that he is alone for the first time. This can be a stressful time for you as well as for the pup. It's important that you remain strong and don't let the puppy out of his crate to comfort him. He will fall asleep eventually. If you release him, the puppy will learn that crying means "out" and will continue that habit. You are laying the groundwork for future habits. Some breeders find that soft music can soothe a crying pup and help him get to sleep.

SOCIALIZING YOUR PUPPY

The first 20 weeks of your Spinone puppy's life are the most important of his entire lifetime. A properly socialized puppy will grow up to be a confident and stable adult who will be a pleasure to live with and a welcome addition to the neighborhood. The importance of socialization cannot be overemphasized. Research on canine behavior has proven that puppies

the neighborhood. Because the Spinone is such a remarkable breed, people will enjoy meeting "the new *bambino* on the block." Take him for short walks, to the park and to other dog-friendly places where he will encounter new people, especially children. Puppies automatically recognize children as "little people" and are drawn to play with them. Just make sure that you supervise these meetings and that the children do not get too rough or encourage him to play too hard. An overzealous pup can often nip

Socialization—that is, introducing your pup around the neighborhood—will bring him out of his shell and make him an outgoing, confident young dog, typical of the breed.

who are not exposed to new sights, sounds, people and animals during their first 20 weeks of life will grow up to be timid and fearful, even aggressive, and unable to flourish outside of their familiar home environment.

Socializing your puppy is not difficult and, in fact, will be a fun time for you both. Lead training goes hand in hand with socialization, so your puppy will be learning how to walk on a lead at the same time that he's meeting

TEMPERAMENT ABOVE ALL ELSE

Regardless of breed, a puppy's disposition is perhaps his most important quality. It is, after all, what makes a puppy lovable and "livable." If the puppy's parents or grandparents are known to be snappy or aggressive, atypical of the Spinone, the puppy is likely to inherit those tendencies. That can lead to serious problems, such as the dog's becoming a biter, which can lead to eventual abandonment.

too hard, frightening the child and in turn making the puppy overly excited. A bad experience in puppyhood can impact a dog for life, so a pup that has a negative experience with a child may grow up to be shy or even aggressive around children.

Take your puppy along on your daily errands. Puppies are natural "people magnets," and most people who see your pup will want to pet him. All of these encounters will help to mold him into a confident adult dog. Likewise, you will soon feel like a confident, responsible dog owner, rightly proud of your well-mannered Spinone.

Be especially careful of your puppy's encounters and experiences during the eight- to ten-week-old period, which is also called the "fear period." This is a

serious imprinting period, and all contact during this time should be gentle and positive. A frightening or negative event could leave a permanent impression that could affect his future behavior if a similar situation arises.

Also make sure that your puppy has received his first and second rounds of vaccinations before you expose him to other dogs or bring him to places that other dogs may frequent. Avoid dog parks and other strange-dog areas until your vet assures you that your puppy is fully immunized and resistant to the diseases that can be passed between canines. Discuss socialization with your breeder, as some breeders recommend socializing the puppy even before he has received all of his inoculations, depending on how outgoing the breed or individual puppy may be.

LEADER OF THE PUPPY'S PACK
Like other canines, your puppy needs an authority figure, someone he can look up to and regard as the leader of his "pack." His first pack leader was his dam, who taught him to be polite and not chew too hard on her ears or nip at her muzzle. He learned those same lessons from his littermates. If he played too rough, they cried in pain and stopped the game, which sent an important message to the rowdy puppy.

As puppies play together, they

are also struggling to determine who will be the boss. Being pack animals, dogs need someone to be in charge. If a litter of puppies remained together beyond puppyhood, one of the pups would emerge as the strongest one, the one who calls the shots.

THE FAMILY FELINE

A resident cat has feline squatter's rights. The cat will treat the newcomer (your puppy) as she sees fit, regardless of what you do or say. So it's best to let the two of them work things out on their own terms. Cats have a height advantage and will generally leap to higher ground to avoid direct contact with a rambunctious pup. Some will hiss and boldly swat at a pup who passes by or tries to reach the cat. Keep the puppy under control in the presence of the cat and they will eventually become accustomed to each other.

Here's a hint: move the cat's litter box where the puppy can't get into it! It's best to do so well before the pup comes home so the cat is used to the new location.

Once your puppy leaves the pack, he will look intuitively for a new leader. If he does not recognize you as that leader, he will try to assume that position for himself. Of course, it is hard to imagine your adorable Spinone puppy trying to be in charge when he is so small and seemingly helpless. You must remember that these are natural canine instincts. Do not cave in and allow your pup to get the upper "paw"!

Just as socialization is so important during these first 20 weeks, so too is your puppy's early education. He was born without any bad habits. He does not know what is good or bad behavior. If he does things like nipping and digging, it's because he is having fun and doesn't know that humans consider these things as "bad." It's your job to teach him proper puppy manners, and this is the best time to accomplish that...before he has developed bad habits, since it is much more difficult to "unlearn" or correct unacceptable learned behavior than to teach good behavior from the start.

Make sure that all members of the family understand the importance of being consistent when training their new puppy. If you tell the puppy to stay off the sofa and your daughter allows him to cuddle on the couch to watch her favorite television show, your pup will be confused about what

BE CONSISTENT

Consistency is a key element, in fact is absolutely necessary, to a puppy's learning environment. A behavior (such as chewing, jumping up or climbing onto the furniture) cannot be forbidden one day and then allowed the next. That will only confuse the pup, and he will not understand what he is supposed to do. Just one or two episodes of allowing an undesirable behavior to "slide" will imprint that behavior on a puppy's brain and make that behavior more difficult to erase or change.

he is and is not allowed to do. Have a family conference before your pup comes home so that everyone understands the basic principles of puppy training and the rules you have set forth for the pup and agrees to follow them.

The old saying that "an ounce of prevention is worth a pound of cure" is especially true when it comes to puppies. It is much

Your pup's special area, with soft bedding so that he can cuddle up, will help him settle into his new home.

easier to prevent inappropriate behavior than it is to change it. It's also easier and less stressful for the pup, since it will keep discipline to a minimum and create a more positive learning environment for him. That, in turn, will also be easier on you!

Here are a few commonsense tips to keep your belongings safe and your puppy out of trouble:

- Keep your closet doors closed and your shoes, socks and other apparel off the floor so your puppy can't get at them.
- Keep a secure lid on the trash container or put the trash where your puppy can't dig into it. He can't damage what he can't reach!
- Supervise your puppy at all times to make sure he is not getting into mischief. If he starts to chew the corner of the rug, you can distract him instantly by tossing a toy for him to fetch. You also will be able to whisk him outside when you notice that he is about to piddle on the carpet. If you can't see your puppy, you can't teach him or correct his behavior.

SOLVING PUPPY PROBLEMS

CHEWING AND NIPPING

Nipping at fingers and toes is normal puppy behavior. Chewing is also the way that puppies investigate their surroundings. However, you will have to teach your puppy that chewing anything other than his toys is not acceptable. That won't happen overnight, and at times puppy teeth will test your patience. However, if you allow nipping and chewing to continue, just think about the damage that a mature Spinone can do with a full set of adult teeth.

Whenever your puppy nips your hand or fingers, cry out "Ouch!" in a loud voice, which should startle your puppy and stop him from nipping, even if only for a moment. Immediately distract him by offering a small treat or an appropriate toy for him to chew instead (which means having chew toys and puppy treats handy or in your pockets at all times). Praise him when he takes the toy and tell him what a good fellow he is. Praise is just as or even more important in puppy training as discipline and correction.

Puppies also tend to nip at children more often than adults, since they perceive little ones to be more vulnerable and more similar to their littermates. Teach your children appropriate responses to nipping behavior. If they are unable to handle it themselves, you may have to intervene. Puppy nips can be quite painful and a child's frightened reaction will only encourage a puppy to nip harder, which is a natural canine response. As with all other puppy situations, interaction between your Spinone puppy and children should be supervised.

Chewing on objects, not just family members' fingers and ankles, is also normal canine behavior that can be especially tedious (for the owner, not the pup) during the teething period when the puppy's adult teeth are coming in. At this stage, chewing just plain feels good. Furniture legs and cabinet corners are common puppy favorites. Shoes and other personal items also taste pretty good to a pup.

The best solution is, once again, prevention. If you value something, keep it tucked away and out of reach. You can't hide your dining-room table in a closet, but you can try to deflect the chewing by applying a bitter product made just to deter dogs from chewing. Available in a spray or cream, this substance is vile-tasting, although safe for dogs, and most puppies will avoid

ESTABLISH A ROUTINE
Routine is very important to a puppy's learning environment. To facilitate house-training, use the same exit/entrance door for potty trips and always take the puppy to the same place in the yard. The same principle of consistency applies to all other aspects of puppy training.

GOOD CHEWING

Chew toys run the gamut from rawhide chews to hard sterile bones and everything in between. Rawhides are all-time favorites, but they can cause choking when they become mushy from repeated chewing, causing them to break into small pieces that are easy to swallow. Rawhides are also highly indigestible, so many vets advise limiting rawhide treats. Hard sterile bones are great for plaque prevention as well as chewing satisfaction. Dispose of them when the ends become sharp or splintered.

the forbidden object after one tiny taste. You also can apply the product to your leather leash if the puppy tries to chew on his lead during leash-training sessions.

Keep a ready supply of safe chews handy to offer your Spinone as a distraction when he starts to chew on something that's a "no-no" and praise him when he chews on the acceptable item. Remember, at this tender age he does not yet know what is permitted or forbidden, so you have to be "on call" every minute he's awake and on the prowl.

Spinone puppies need to chew, so give the pup plenty of toys and keep your shoes in a safe place!

You may lose a treasure or two during the puppy's growing-up period, and the furniture could sustain a nasty nick or two. These can be trying times, so be prepared for those inevitable accidents and comfort yourself in knowing that this too shall pass.

PUPPY WHINING

Puppies often cry and whine, just as infants and little children do. It's their way of telling us that they are lonely or in need of attention. Your puppy will miss his littermates and will feel insecure when he is left alone. You may be out of the house or just in another room, but he will still feel alone. During these times, the puppy's crate should be his personal comfort station, a place all his own where he can feel safe and secure. Once he learns that being alone is okay

HAPPY PUPPIES COME RUNNING

Never call your puppy (or adult dog) to come to you and then scold him or discipline him when he gets there. He will make a natural association between coming to you and being scolded, and he will think he was a bad dog for coming to you. He will then be reluctant to come whenever he is called. Always praise your puppy every time he comes to you.

and not something to be feared, he will settle down without crying or objecting. You might want to leave a radio on while he is crated, as the sound of human voices can be soothing and will give the impression that people are around.

Give your puppy a sturdy toy to entertain him whenever he is crated. You will both be happier: the puppy because he is safe in his den and you because he is quiet, safe and not getting into puppy escapades that can wreak havoc in your house or cause him danger.

To make sure that your puppy will always view his crate as a safe and cozy place, never, *ever* use the crate as punishment. That's the best way to turn the crate into a negative place that the pup will want to avoid. Sure, you can use the crate for your own peace of mind if your puppy is getting into trouble and needs some "time out." Just don't let him know that! Never scold the pup and immediately place him into the crate. Count to ten, give him a couple of hugs and maybe a treat, then scoot him into his crate.

It's also important not to make a big fuss when he is released from the crate. That will make getting out of the crate more appealing than being in the crate, which is just the opposite of what you are trying to achieve.

SPINONE ITALIANO

Adding a Spinone Italiano to your household means adding a new family member who will need your care each and every day. When your Spinone pup first comes home, you will start a routine with him so that, as he grows up, your dog will have a daily schedule just as you do. The aspects of your dog's daily care will likewise become regular parts of your day, so you'll both have a new schedule. Dogs learn by consistency and thrive on routine: regular times for meals, exercise, grooming and potty trips are just as important for your dog as they are for you! Your dog's schedule will depend much on your family's daily routine, but remember that you now have a new member of the family who is part of your day every day.

FEEDING YOUR SPINONE
If you ask a Spinone breeder or owner what and when you should feed your new puppy, he will surely tell you that a specific feeding schedule is critical and that a good rule of thumb is to feed the amount that the puppy, or adult for that matter, will eat in

five minutes. (If you were to ask a Spinone that same question, the answer would undoubtedly be "everything and always!") The recommended content may vary from breeder to breeder, but the five-minute rule is likely to remain constant.

Unlike the advice given to the new owners of many other breeds, the Spinone's food intake must be

VARIETY IS THE SPICE
Although dog-food manufacturers contend that dogs don't like variety in their diets, studies show quite the opposite to be true. Dogs would much rather vary their meals than eat the same old chow day in and day out. Dry kibble is no more exciting for a dog than the same bowl of bran flakes would be for you. Fortunately, there are dozens of varieties available on the market, and your dog will likely show preference for certain flavors over others. A word of warning: don't overdo it or you'll develop a fussy eater who only prefers chopped beef fillet and asparagus tips every night.

regulated carefully because Spinoni are hungry around the clock, and in most cases hungry for anything that even remotely resembles food! An overweight puppy or dog can quickly become the result. This puts stress on the kidneys and heart, to say nothing of the strain on a puppy's susceptible skeletal development. A feeding schedule also allows you to give the dog adequate rest time before and after meals, essential to bloat prevention.

After weaning and up to about three months of age, the Spinone puppy should be getting four meals a day. At that point, three meals a day are sufficient and, by the time the puppy is six months old, he might well be put on a morning/evening schedule. Here again, these are simply rules of thumb. The lean and leggy puppy might need a supplement to the morning/evening schedule. The too-pudgy puppy should be kept on the two-meal schedule, but perhaps fed a bit less at each.

Most breeders recommend keeping the Spinone on puppy food until about six to seven months of age. Depending upon individual dog and general condition (weight, activity, etc.), an active Spinone should be able to stay on a maintenance diet until he reaches that "slow-down" point in his life; he then can be switched to a senior diet. Again, this varies from dog to dog.

Mangia, cane: Italian through and through, Spinoni love dinnertime! Don't give in to the heritage, and avoid pasta at all costs.

Most commercial foods manufactured for dogs meet nutrition standards and list the ingredients contained in the food on every package and can. The ingredients are listed in descending order, with the main ingredient listed first. Refined sugars are not a part of the canine natural food acquisition, and canine teeth are not genetically disposed to handling these sugars. Do not feed your Spinone sugar products, and avoid products that contain sugar to any high degree.

Fresh water and a properly prepared, balanced diet containing the essential nutrients in correct proportions are all that a healthy Spinone needs to be offered. Dog foods come canned, dry, semi-moist, "scientifically fortified,"

From birth to first taste of mother's milk...the photo shows the puppy being born in a placenta-filled sac.

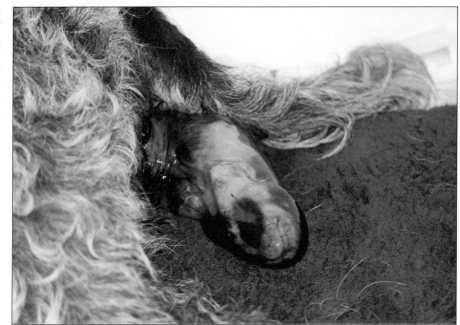

The mother bites through the umbilical cord to release the pup from the sac.

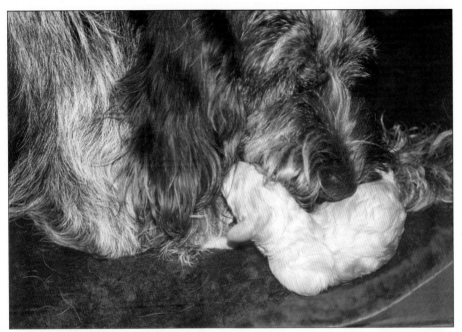

After eating the placenta, the dam licks the puppy dry.

Three minutes after birth, the puppy's eyes are not yet opened.

The pups seek out the mother's nipples and begin to suckle.

Mom and her newborn litter of hungry pups.

As the pups mature, the breeder introduces solid food as part of the weaning process.

"all-natural" and more! A visit to your local pet store will reveal how vast an array you will be able to select from.

All dogs, whether large or small, are carnivorous (meat-eating) animals. Animal protein and fats are essential to the well-being of your Spinone. However, a diet too high in proteins can lead to problems as well. Not all dry foods contain the necessary amount of protein that a Spinone requires to keep him in top condition. It is best to discuss this with the breeder from whom you purchase your dog or with your veterinarian.

The domesticated dog's diet must include protein, carbohydrates, fats, roughage and small amounts of essential minerals and vitamins. Many breeders strongly recommend adding small amounts of cooked vegetables to a Spinone's diet. This provides the necessary carbohydrates, minerals and nutrients present only in vegetables.

Commercially prepared foods contain all of the necessary vitamins your Spinone needs. It is unnecessary, in fact inadvisable, to add vitamin supplements to these diets in other than special circumstances prescribed by your veterinarian. Over-supplementation and forced growth are now looked upon by some breeders as major contributors to many skeletal abnormalities found in pure-bred dogs of the day. Some people may claim these problems and a wide variety of chronic skin conditions are entirely hereditary, but many

others feel they can be exacer-
bated by diet and over-use of
mineral and vitamin supplements
for puppies.

**TYPES OF FOOD AND READING THE
LABEL**
When selecting the type of food
to feed your dog, it is important
to check out the label for ingredients. Many dry-food products
have soybean, corn or rice as the
main ingredient. The main
ingredient will be listed first on
the label, with the rest of the
ingredients following in
descending order according to
their proportion in the food.
While these types of dry food are
acceptable, you should look into
dry foods based on meat or fish.
These are better-quality foods
and thus higher priced. However,
they may be just as economical
in the long run, because studies
have shown that it takes less of
the higher-quality foods to
maintain a dog.

Comparing the various types
of food, dry, canned and semi-
moist, dry foods contain the least
amount of water and canned
foods the most. Proportionately,
dry foods are the most calorie-
and nutrient-dense, which means
that you need more of a canned
food product to supply the same
amount of nutrition. In
households with breeds of
different size, the canned/dry/
semi-moist question can be of

special importance. Larger breeds
obviously eat more than smaller
ones and thus in general do
better on dry foods, but smaller
breeds do fine on canned foods
and require "small bite" formulations to protect their small
mouths and teeth if fed dry
foods. So if you have breeds of
different sizes in your home,
consider both your own prefer-
ences and what your dogs like to
eat, but in the main think canned
for the little guys and dry or
semi-moist for everyone else. You
may find success mixing the food
types as well. Water is important

for all dogs, but even more so for those fed dry foods, as there is no high water content in their food.

There are strict controls that regulate the nutritional content of dog food, and a food has to meet the minimum requirements in order to be considered "complete and balanced." It is important that you choose such a food for your dog, so check the label to be sure that your chosen food meets the requirements. If not, look for a food that clearly states on the label that it is formulated to be complete and

THE DARK SIDE OF CHOCOLATE

From a tiny chip to a giant rabbit, chocolate—in any form—is not your dog's friend. Whether it's an Oreo® cookie, a Snickers® bar or even a couple of M&M's®, your dog must not be allowed access to these items. You are also well advised to avoid any bone toy that is made out of fake chocolate or any treat made of carob—anything that encourages your dog to become a "chocoholic" can't be helpful. Before you toss your pooch half of your candy bar, consider that as little as a single ounce of chocolate can poison a 30-pound dog. Theobromine, like caffeine, is a methylxanthine and occurs naturally in cocoa beans. Dogs metabolize theobromine very slowly, and its effect on the dog can be serious, harming the heart, kidneys and central nervous system. Dark or semi-sweet chocolate is even worse than milk chocolate, and baking chocolate and cocoa mix are by far the worst.

Food is number one on the Spinone's list of priorities, and if there's food to be found, he will find it and help himself! Keep "people food" out of the dog's reach—food stealing is neither good behavior nor good for the dog.

balanced for your dog's particular stage of life.

Recommendations for amounts to feed will also be indicated on the label. You should also ask your vet about proper food portions, and you will need to keep an eye on your dog's condition to see whether the recommended amounts are adequate. If he becomes over- or underweight, you will need to make adjustments; this also would be a good time to consult your veterinarian.

The food label may also make feeding suggestions, such as

QUENCHING HIS THIRST

Is your dog drinking more than normal and trying to lap up everything in sight? Excessive drinking has many different causes. Obvious causes for a dog's being thirstier than usual are hot weather and vigorous exercise. However, if your dog is drinking more for no apparent reason, you could have cause for concern. Serious conditions like kidney or liver disease, diabetes and various types of hormonal problems can all be indicated by excessive drinking. If you notice your dog's being excessively thirsty, contact your vet at once. Hopefully there will be a simpler explanation, but the earlier a serious problem is detected, the sooner it can be treated, with a better rate of cure.

whether moistening a dry-food product is recommended. A splash of water can help a "chow hound" eat more slowly, thus aiding in bloat prevention. Don't be overwhelmed by the many factors that go into feeding your dog. Manufacturers of complete and balanced foods make it easy, and once you find the right food and amounts for your Spinone, his daily feeding will be a matter of routine.

DON'T FORGET THE WATER!

There's no doubt that your Spinone needs plenty of water. Fresh cold water, in a clean bowl, should be available to your dog indoors and out. There are special circumstances, such as during puppy housebreaking, when you will want to monitor your pup's water intake so that you will be able to predict when he will need to relieve himself, but water must be available to him nonetheless. Water is essential for hydration and proper body function just as it is in humans.

You will get to know how much your dog typically drinks in a day. Of course, in the heat or if exercising vigorously, he will be more thirsty and will drink more. However, if he begins to drink noticeably more water for no apparent reason, this could signal any of various problems, and you are advised to consult your vet.

Water is the best drink for dogs. Some owners are tempted to give milk from time to time or to moisten dry food with milk, but dogs do not have the enzymes necessary to digest the lactose in milk, which is much different from the milk that nursing puppies receive. Therefore, stick with clean fresh water to quench your dog's thirst, and always have it readily available to him.

A word of caution concerning your deep-chested dog's water intake: he should never be allowed to gulp water, especially at mealtimes. In fact, water should not be offered at mealtimes as a rule. This simple daily precaution can go a long way in protecting your dog from the dangerous and potentially fatal gastric torsion (bloat).

EXERCISE

Exercise is a bottom-line fact in a Spinone's life. The Spinone was bred to work day in and day out in the field, and that ability and

Water is as necessary to the dog's well-being as his diet, but a Spinone should never be allowed to gulp water.

A Spinone working the field is poetry in motion, and exercise like this is an absolute necessity for this sporting breed.

need remain with the breed to this day. A well-exercised Spinone can live happily with just a reasonably-sized run in a big city, but understand the operative words here are "well-exercised." That means full-out running (under your control, keeping safety in mind) on the beach or in the country several times a week at the very minimum. Do not expect that a short gallop in the park will suffice. If it is to be the park where your Spinone will get his exercise, consider who will keep an eye out for toddlers or "little fluffies" who are going about their own business. Particularly when the Spinone is running free, those little objects entice him to give chase.

Mature Spinoni are capable and delighted to be jogging companions. It is important, however, to use good judgment in any exercise program. Begin slowly and increase the distance to be covered very gradually over an extended period of time. Use special precautions in hot weather. High temperatures and forced exercise are a dangerous combination.

Since the growing frames of young dogs are susceptible to injury, puppies should never be forced to exercise. Normally, they are little dynamos of energy and keep themselves busy all day long, interspersed with frequent naps. Never expose puppies to strenuous activities or exercise.

The best exercise for a Spinone is that which he acquires in the pursuit of the very thing the breed

Use of a grooming table raises the dog to a comfortable height for the groomer to work, while keeping the dog secure and still during the process.

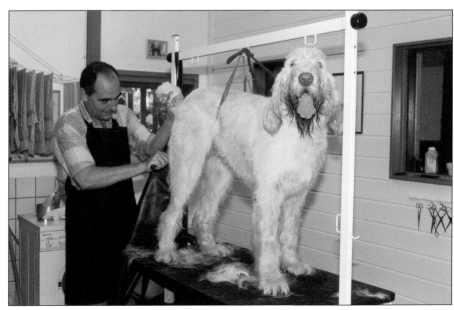

was created for—field work. There is no better way to ensure your Spinone of a happy, healthy existence.

GROOMING YOUR SPINONE

BRUSHING AND COAT MAINTENANCE
The Spinone is a natural breed that requires only minor clipping and neatening around the tail, legs and feet. Thinning shears are excellent for this purpose. Invest in a quality pair of thinning shears, a slicker or pin brush and a good natural bristle brush that has some nylon bristles inserted in it. You will also need a steel comb to remove any debris that collects in the longer furnishings. A comb that has teeth divided between fine and coarse is ideal. All of these supplies are available at the local pet-supply shop.

Regular thorough brushing with the slicker or pin brush to keep the coat and furnishings tangle-free should be part of a regular routine. Follow this with a stimulating brush-down with the bristle brush. Together, those operations will keep both the coat and skin clean and healthy.

The longer hair of the ears and beard will attract food and debris. Use a metal comb especially for dogs for this purpose. Frequent bathing is suggested for these two areas. This will keep debris from collecting and avoid foul smells from developing. You can dry-

bathe your Spinone by sprinkling a little baby powder in the coat and then working it well in and brushing it out. This, of course, also helps to make the dog smell very good. Over-bathing can lead to dry-skin problems. Dry skin creates a need to scratch and this can lead to severe scratching and "hot spots," moist sore areas in which the coat is entirely scratched away.

The easiest way to groom a Spinone is by placing the dog on a grooming table or elevated platform. Make sure the dog is at a height at which you can work comfortably either sitting or standing. Adjustable-height grooming tables are available at most pet-supply outlets and are well worth the initial investment. It is best to use a grooming table that has an "arm" and a "noose." The noose is attached to the arm; it slips around the dog's neck when

Every part of the Spinone should be groomed, even the sensitive areas, which require careful and gentle attention.

one of the specially prepared grooming powders directly to the mat and brush completely from the skin out. If a mat or tangle should develop and you find you can't work it apart with your fingers and a steel comb, use the thinning shears to help separate the mat.

The coat of a neutered or spayed Spinone will be softer and longer than that of an unaltered dog. It is helpful to strip the coat of an altered Spinone two or three time a year to keep the coat harsher and in a more natural prickly state. A stripping knife is used for this purpose, and the breeder from which the Spinone is purchased can instruct almost any owner how to accomplish the procedure.

BATHING

In general, dogs need to be bathed only a few times a year, possibly more often if your dog gets into something messy or if he starts to smell like a dog. Show dogs are usually bathed more frequently, although this depends on the owner. Bathing too frequently can have negative effects on the skin and coat, removing natural oils and causing dryness.

If you give your dog his first bath when he is young, he will become accustomed to the process. Wrestling a dog into the tub or chasing a freshly shampooed dog who has escaped from the bath will be no fun! Most

Hand-stripping is an art that takes time and practice to learn and perfect.

he is standing and keeps the dog from fidgeting about or jumping down when he has decided he has had enough grooming. However, do not leave your dog alone when you are using the noose, even for a a minute. Your dog could jump or fall off the table and injure himself.

When brushing, proceed vigorously from behind the head to the tail. Do this all over the body and be especially careful to attend to the hard-to-reach areas between the legs, behind the ears and under the body. Mats can occur, particularly when the dog is shedding or when the coat catches burs or sticky substances in its longer furnishings. Should you encounter a mat that does not brush out easily, use your fingers and the steel comb to separate the hairs as much as possible. Apply baby powder or

SELECTING THE RIGHT BRUSHES AND COMBS

Will a rubber curry make my dog look slicker? Is a rake smaller than a pin brush? Do I choose nylon or natural bristles? Buying a dog brush can make the hairs on your head stand on end! Here's a quick once-over to educate you on the different types of brushes.

Slicker Brush: Fine metal prongs closely set on a curved base. Used to remove dead coat from the undercoat of medium- to long-coated breeds.

Pin Brush: Metal pins, often covered with rubber tips, set on an oval base. Used to remove shedding hair and is gentler than a slicker brush.

Metal Comb: Steel teeth attached to a steel handle; the closeness and size of the teeth vary greatly. A "flea comb" has tiny teeth set very closely together and is used to find fleas in a dog's coat. Combs with wider teeth are used for detangling longer coats.

Rake: Long-toothed comb with a short handle. Used to remove undercoat from heavily coated breeds with dense undercoats.

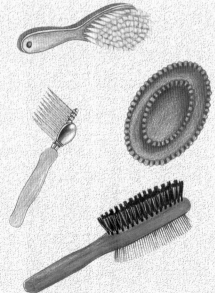

Soft-bristle Brush: Nylon or natural bristles set in a plastic or wood base. Used on short coats or long coats (without undercoats).

Rubber Curry: Rubber prongs, with or without a handle. Used for short-coated dogs. Good for use during shampooing.

Combination Brushes: Two-sided brush with a different type of bristle on each side; for example, pin brush on one side and slicker on the other, or bristle brush on one side and pin brush on the other. An economical choice if you need two kinds of brushes.

Grooming Glove: Sometimes called a hound glove; used to give sleek-coated dogs a once-over.

WATER SHORTAGE
Pet shops sell excellent products, in both powder and spray forms, designed for spot-cleaning your dog. These dry shampoos are convenient for touch-up jobs when you don't have the time to bathe your dog in the traditional way. Muddy feet, messy behinds and smelly coats can be spot-cleaned and deodorized with a "wet-nap"-style cleaner. On those days when your dog insists on rolling in fresh goose droppings and there's no time for a bath, a spot bath can save the day. These pre-moistened wipes are also handy for other grooming needs like wiping faces, ears and eyes and freshening tails and behinds.

dogs don't naturally enjoy their baths, but you at least want yours to cooperate with you.

Before bathing the dog, have the items you'll need close at hand. First, decide where you will bathe the dog. You should have a tub or basin with a non-slip surface. Puppies can even be bathed in a sink. In warm weather, some like to use a portable pool in the yard, although you'll want to make sure your dog doesn't head for the nearest dirt pile following his bath! You will also need a hose or shower spray to wet the coat thoroughly, a shampoo formulated for dogs, absorbent towels and perhaps a blow dryer. Human shampoos are too harsh for dogs'

coats and will dry them out.

Before wetting the dog, give him a brush-through to remove any dead hair, dirt and mats. Make sure he is at ease in the tub and have the water at a comfortable temperature. Begin bathing by wetting the coat all the way down to the skin. Massage in the shampoo, keeping it away from his face and eyes. Rinse him thoroughly, again avoiding the eyes and ears, as you don't want to get water into the ear canals. A thorough rinsing is important, as shampoo residue is drying and itchy to the dog. After rinsing, wrap him in a towel to absorb the initial moisture. You can finish drying with either a towel or a blow dryer on low heat, held at a safe distance from the dog. You should keep the dog indoors and away from drafts until he is completely dry.

NAIL CLIPPING

Having his nails trimmed is not on many dogs' lists of favorite things to do. With this in mind, you will need to accustom your puppy to the procedure at a young age so that he will sit still (well, as still as he can) for his pedicures. Long nails can cause the dog's feet to spread, which is not good for him; likewise, long nails can hurt if they unintentionally scratch, not good for you!

Some dogs' nails are worn down naturally by regular walking

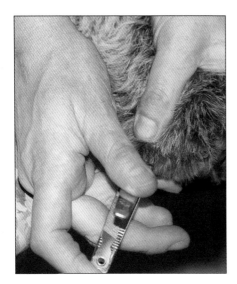

the nail tip is inserted into the opening, and blades on the top and bottom snip it off in one clip.

Start by grasping the pup's paw; a little pressure on the foot pad causes the nail to extend, making it easier to clip. Clip off a little at a time. If you can see the "quick," which is a blood vessel that runs through each nail, you will know how much to trim, as you do not want to cut into the

on hard surfaces, so the frequency with which you clip depends on your individual dog. Look at his nails from time to time and clip as needed; a good way to know when it's time for a trim is if you hear your dog clicking as he walks across the floor.

There are several types of nail clippers and even electric nail-grinding tools made for dogs. First we'll discuss using the clipper. To start, have your clipper ready and some doggie treats on hand. You want your pup to view his nail-clipping sessions in a positive light, and what better way to convince him than with food? You may want to enlist the help of an assistant to comfort the pup and offer treats as you concentrate on the clipping itself. The guillo-tine-type clipper is thought of by many as the easiest type to use;

If nail clipping is part of the grooming routine starting in puppyhood, your Spinone should tolerate his pedicures.

SCOOTING HIS BOTTOM

Here's a doggy problem that many owners tend to neglect. If your dog is scooting his rear end around the carpet, he probably is experiencing anal-sac impaction or blockage. The anal sacs are the two grape-sized glands on either side of the dog's vent, and if the dog cannot empty these glands, they will fill with a foul-smelling material. The dog may attempt to lick the area to relieve the pressure. He may also rub his anus on your walls, furniture or floors.

Don't neglect your dog's rear end during grooming sessions. By squeezing both sides of the anus with a soft cloth, you can express some of the material in the sacs. If the material is pasty and thick, you likely will need the assistance of a veterinarian. Vets know how to express the glands and can show you how to do it correctly without hurting the dog or spraying yourself with the unpleasant liquid.

THE MONTHLY GRIND

If your dog doesn't like the feeling of nail clippers or if you're not comfortable using them, you may wish to try an electric nail grinder. This tool has a small sandpaper disc on the end that rotates to grind the nails down. Some feel that using a grinder reduces the risk of cutting into the quick; this can be true if the tool is used properly. Usually you will be able to tell where the quick is before you get to it. A benefit of the grinder is that it creates a smooth finish on the nails so that there are no ragged edges.

Because the tool makes noise, your dog should be introduced to it before the actual grinding takes place. Turn it on and let your dog hear the noise; turn it off and let him inspect it with you holding it. Use the grinder gently, holding it firmly and progressing a little at a time until you reach the proper length. Look at the nail as you grind so that you do not go too short. Stop at any indication that you are nearing the quick. It will take a few sessions for both you and the puppy to get used to the grinder. Make sure that you don't let his hair get tangled in the grinder!

or fuss, as this will cause the pup to be afraid. Simply reassure the pup, stop the bleeding and move on to the next nail. Don't be discouraged; you will become a professional canine pedicurist with practice.

You may or may not be able to see the quick, so it's best to just clip off a small bit at a time. If you see a dark dot in the center of the nail, this is the quick and your cue to stop clipping. Tell the puppy he's a "good boy" and offer a piece of treat with each nail. You can also use nail-clipping time to examine the footpads, making sure that they are not dry and cracked and that nothing has become embedded in them.

The nail grinder, the second choice, is many owners' first choice. Accustoming the puppy to the sound of the grinder and sensation of the buzz presents fewer challenges than the clipper, and there's no chance of cutting through the quick. Use the grinder on a low setting and always talk soothingly to your dog. He won't mind his salon visit, and he'll have nicely polished nails as well.

EAR CLEANING

While keeping your Spinone's ears clean will not cause him to "hear" your commands any better, it will protect him from ear infection and ear-mite infestation. In addition, a dog's ears are vulnerable to waxy build-up and to collecting foreign

quick. On that note, if you do cut the quick, which will cause bleeding, you can stem the flow of blood with a styptic pencil or other clotting agent. If you mistakenly nip the quick, do not panic

matter from the outdoors. Look in your dog's ears regularly to ensure that they look pink, clean and otherwise healthy. Even if they look fine, an odor in the ears signals a problem and means it's time to call the vet.

A dog's ears should be cleaned regularly; once a week is suggested, and you can do this along with your regular brushing. Using a cotton ball or pad, and never probing into the ear canal, wipe the ear gently. You can use an ear-cleansing liquid or powder available from your vet or pet-supply store; alternatively, you might prefer to use home-made solutions with ingredients like one part white vinegar and one part hydrogen peroxide. Ask your vet about home remedies before you attempt to concoct something on your own!

Keep your dog's ears free of excess hair by plucking it as needed. If done gently, this will be painless for the dog. Look for wax, brown droppings (a sign of ear mites), redness or any other abnormalities. At the first sign of a problem, contact your vet so that he can prescribe an appropriate medication.

Eye Care

During grooming sessions, pay extra attention to the condition of your dog's eyes. If the area around the eyes is soiled or if tear staining has occurred, there are various cleaning agents made especially for this purpose. Look at the dog's eyes to make sure no debris has entered; dogs with large eyes and those who spend much time outdoors are especially prone to this.

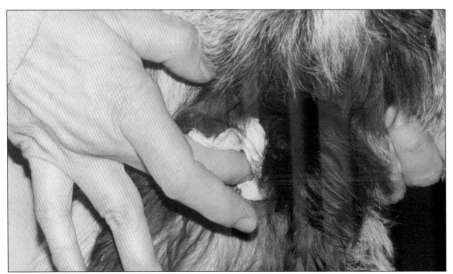

Use a soft cotton wipe to clean your Spinone's ears. Pet-supply stores or your vet can offer suitable ear-cleaning solutions.

The signs of an eye infection are obvious: mucus, redness, puffiness, scabs or other signs of irritation. If your dog's eyes become infected, the vet will likely prescribe an antibiotic ointment for treatment. If you notice signs of more serious problems, such as opacities in the eye, which usually indicate cataracts, consult the vet at once. Taking time to pay attention to your dog's eyes will alert you in the early stages of any problem so that you can get your dog treatment as soon as possible. You could save your dog's sight!

A CLEAN SMILE

Another essential part of grooming is brushing your dog's teeth and checking his overall oral condition. Studies show that around 80% of dogs experience dental problems by two years of age, and the percentage is higher in older dogs. Therefore, it is highly likely that your dog will have trouble with his teeth and gums unless you are proactive with home dental care.

The most common dental problem in dogs is plaque build-up. If not treated, this causes gum disease, infection and resultant tooth loss. Bacteria from these infections spread throughout the body, affecting the vital organs. Do you need much more convincing to start brushing your dog's teeth? If so, take a good whiff of your dog's breath and read on.

Fortunately, home dental care is rather easy and convenient for pet owners. Specially formulated canine toothpaste is easy to find. You should use one of these toothpastes, not a product for humans. Some doggie pastes are even available in flavors appealing to dogs. If your dog likes the flavor, he will tolerate the process better, making things much easier for you! Doggie toothbrushes come in different sizes and are designed to fit the contour of a canine mouth. Rubber fingertip brushes fit right on one of your fingers and have rubber nodes to clean the teeth and massage the gums. This may be easier to handle, as it is akin to rubbing your dog's teeth with your finger.

Brushing your dog's teeth is an essential facet of his proper healthcare. Many serious problems can stem from a lack of effective dental care.

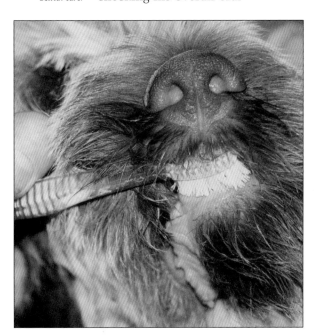

As with other grooming tasks, accustom your Spinone pup to his dental care early on. Start gently, for a few minutes at a time, so that he gets used to the feel of the brush and to your handling his mouth. Offer praise and petting so that he looks at tooth-care time as a time when he gets extra love and attention. The routine should become second nature; he may not like it, but he should at least tolerate it.

Aside from brushing, offer dental toys to your dog and feed crunchy biscuits, which help to minimize plaque. Rope toys have the added benefit of acting like floss as the dog chews. At your adult dog's yearly check-ups, the vet will likely perform a thorough tooth scraping as well as a complete check for any problems. Proper care of your dog's teeth will ensure that you will enjoy your dog's smile for many years to come. The next time your dog goes to give you a hello kiss, you'll be glad you spent the time caring for his teeth.

ID FOR YOUR DOG

You love your Spinone and want to keep him safe. Of course you take every precaution to prevent his escaping from the yard or becoming lost or stolen. You have a sturdy high fence and you always keep your dog on lead when out and about in public places. If your dog is not properly

> ### PET OR STRAY?
> Besides the obvious benefit of providing your contact information to whoever finds your lost dog, an ID tag makes your dog more approachable and more likely to be recovered. A strange dog wandering the neighborhood without a collar and tags will look like a stray, while the collar and tags indicate that the dog is someone's pet. Even if the ID tags become detached from the collar, the collar alone will make a person more likely to pick up the dog.

identified, however, you are overlooking a major aspect of his safety. We hope to never be in a situation where our dog is missing, but we should practice prevention in the unfortunate case that this happens; identification greatly increases the chances of your dog's being returned to you.

There are several ways to identify your dog. First, the traditional dog tag should be a staple in your dog's wardrobe, attached to his everyday collar. Tags can be made of sturdy plastic and various metals and should

Never drive with your Spinone unrestrained in the car. Crates, harnesses and partitions for the back of the vehicle are three safety options available for your dog.

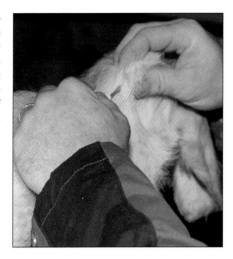

Microchip implantation can be performed by your vet. This is a permanent and reliable method of identifying a dog.

explore the type of tag that slides right onto the collar.

In addition to the ID tag, which every dog should wear even if identified by another method, two other forms of identification have become popular: microchipping and tattooing. In microchipping, a tiny scannable chip is painlessly inserted under the dog's skin. The number is registered to you so that, if your lost dog turns up at a clinic or shelter, the chip can be scanned to retrieve your contact information.

The advantage of the microchip is that it is a permanent form of ID, but there are some factors to consider. Several different companies make microchips, and not all are compatible with the others' scanning devices. It's best to find a company with a universal microchip that can be read by scanners made by other companies as well. It won't do any good to have the dog chipped if the information cannot be retrieved. Also, not every humane society, shelter and clinic is equipped with a scanner, although more and more facilities are equipping themselves. In fact, many shelters microchip dogs that they adopt out to new homes.

include your contact information so that a person who finds the dog can get in touch with you right away to arrange his return. Many people today enjoy the wide range of decorative tags available, so have fun and create a tag to match your dog's personality. Of course, it is important that the tag stays on the collar, so have a secure "O" ring attachment; you also can

In the US, there are five or six major microchip manufacturers as well as a few databases. The AKC's Companion Animal

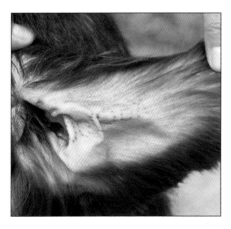

Identification tattoo inside the Spinone's ear flap.

DOGGONE!

Wendy Ballard is the editor and publisher of the *DogGone*™ newsletter, which comes out bi-monthly and features fun articles by dog owners who love to travel with their dogs. The newsletter includes information about fun places to go with your dogs, including popular vacation spots, dog-friendly hotels, parks, campgrounds, resorts, etc., as well as interesting activities to do with your dog, such as flyball, agility and much more. You can subscribe to the publication by contacting the publisher at PO Box 651155, Vero Beach, FL 32965-1155

Recovery unit works in conjunction with HomeAgain™ Companion Animal Retrieval System (Schering-Plough). In the UK, The Kennel Club is affiliated with the National Pet Register, operated by Wood Green Animal Shelters.

Because the microchip is not visible to the eye, the dog must wear a tag that states that he is microchipped so that whoever picks him up will know to have him scanned. He of course also should have a tag with contact information in case his chip cannot be read. Humane societies and veterinary clinics offer microchipping service, which is usually very affordable.

Though less popular than microchipping, tattooing is another permanent method of ID for dogs. Most vets perform this service, and there are also clinics that perform dog tattooing. This is also an affordable procedure and one that will not cause much discomfort for the dog. It is best to put the tattoo in a visible area, such as the ear, to deter theft. It is sad to say that there are cases of dogs' being stolen and sold to research laboratories, but such laboratories will not accept tattooed dogs.

To ensure that the tattoo is effective in aiding your dog's return to you, the tattoo number must be registered with a national organization. That way, when someone finds a tattooed dog, a phone call to the registry will quickly match the dog with his owner.

If your dog is properly identified, it will be much easier to retrieve him if he decides to "hit the road."

SPINONE ITALIANO

BASIC TRAINING PRINCIPLES: PUPPY VS. ADULT

There's a big difference between training an adult dog and training a young puppy. With a young puppy, everything is new. At eight to ten weeks of age, he will be experiencing many things, and he has nothing with which to compare these experiences. Up to this point, he has been with his dam and littermates, not one-on-one with people except in his interactions with his breeder and visitors to the litter.

When you first bring the puppy home, he is eager to please you. This means that he accepts doing things your way. During the next couple of months, he will absorb the basis of everything he needs to know for the rest of his life. This early age is even referred to as the "sponge" stage. After that, for the next 18 months, it's up to you to reinforce good manners by building on the foundation that you've established. Once your puppy is reliable in basic commands and behavior and has reached the appropriate age, you may gradually introduce him to some of the interesting sports, games and activities available to pet owners and their dogs.

Raising your puppy is a family affair. Each member of the family must know what rules to set forth for the puppy and

how to use the same one-word commands to mean exactly the same thing every time. Even if yours is a large family, one person will soon be considered by the pup to be the leader, the Alpha person in his pack, the "boss" who must be obeyed. Often that highly regarded person turns out to be the one who feeds the puppy. Food ranks very high on the Spinone puppy's list of important things! That's why your puppy is

THE RIGHT START

The best advice for a potential dog owner is to start with the very best puppy that money can buy. Don't shop around for a bargain in the newspaper. You're buying a companion, not a used car or a second-hand appliance. The purchase price of the dog represents a very significant part of the investment, but this is indeed a very small sum compared to the expenses of maintaining the dog in good health. If you purchase a well-bred, healthy and sound puppy, you will be starting right. An unhealthy puppy can cost you thousands of dollars in unnecessary veterinary expenses and, possibly, a fortune in heartbreak as well.

The Spinone is an intelligent and loyal breed that responds to its master and to positive methods of training.

rewarded with small treats along with verbal praise when he responds to you correctly. As the puppy learns to do what you want him to do, the food rewards are gradually eliminated and only the praise remains. If you were to keep up with the food treats, you could have two problems on your hands—an obese dog and a beggar.

Training begins the minute your Spinone puppy steps through the doorway of your

home, so don't make the mistake of putting the puppy on the floor and telling him by your actions to "Go for it! Run wild!" Even if this is your first puppy, you must act as if you know what you're doing: be the boss. An uncertain pup may be terrified to move, while a bold one will be ready to take you at your word and start plotting to destroy the house! Before you collected your puppy, you decided where his own special place would be, and that's where to put him when you first arrive home. Give him a house tour after he has investigated his area, had a nap and taken a bathroom "pit stop."

It's worth mentioning here that if you've adopted an adult dog that is completely trained to your liking, lucky you! You're off the hook! However, if that dog spent his life up to this point in a kennel, or even in a good home but without any real training, be prepared to tackle the job ahead. A dog three years of age or older with no previous training cannot be blamed for not knowing what he was never taught. While the dog is trying to understand and learn your rules, at the same time he has to unlearn many of his previously self-taught habits and general view of the world.

Working with a professional trainer will speed up your

progress with an adopted adult dog. You'll need patience, too. Some new rules may be close to impossible for the dog to accept. After all, he's been successful so far by doing everything his way! (Patience again.) He may agree with your instruction for a few days and then slip back into his old ways, so you must be just as consistent and understanding in

A stern word is all that the sensitive Spinone needs as an effective correction.

KEEP IT SIMPLE—AND FUN

Practicing obedience is not a military drill. Keep your lessons simple, interesting and user-friendly. Fun breaks help you both. Spend two minutes or ten teaching your puppy, but practice only as long as your dog enjoys what he's doing and is focused on pleasing you. If he's bored or distracted, stop the training session after any correct response (always end on a high note!). After a few minutes of playtime, you can go back to "hitting the books."

strangers and your friends, and how he acts upon meeting other dogs. If he was not socialized with dogs as a puppy, this could be a major problem. This does not mean that he's a "bad" dog, a vicious dog or an aggressive dog; rather, it means that he has no idea how to read another dog's body language. There's no way for him to tell whether the other dog is a friend or foe. Survival instinct takes over, telling him to attack first and ask questions later. This definitely calls for professional

Puppies have no trouble finding trouble! Defining your pup's living space promotes good behavior in that it lessens the risk of his getting into something he shouldn't.

your teaching as you would be with a puppy. (More patience needed yet again!) Your dog has to learn to pay attention to your voice, your family, the daily routine, new smells, new sounds and, in some cases, even a new climate.

One of the most important things to find out about a newly adopted adult dog is his reaction to children (yours and others),

help and, even then, may not be a behavior that can be corrected 100% reliably (or even at all). If you have a puppy, this is why it is very important to introduce your young puppy properly to other puppies and "dog-friendly" adult dogs.

HOUSE-TRAINING YOUR SPINONE

Dogs are tactility-oriented when it comes to house-training. In other words, they respond to the surface on which they are given approval to eliminate. The choice is yours (the dog's version is in parentheses): The lawn (including the neighbors' lawns)? A bare patch of earth under a tree (where people like to sit and relax in the summer-

> **CREATURES OF HABIT**
> Canine behaviorists and trainers aptly describe dogs as "creatures of habit," meaning that dogs respond to structure in their daily lives and welcome a routine. Do not interpret this to mean that dogs enjoy endless repetition in their training sessions. Dogs get bored just as humans do. Keep training sessions interesting and exciting. Vary the commands and the locations in which you practice. Give short breaks for play in between lessons. A bored student will never be the best performer in the class.

time)? Concrete steps or patio (all sidewalks, garage and basement floors)? The curbside (watch out for cars)? A small area of crushed stone in a corner of the yard (mine!)? The latter is the best choice if you can manage it, because it will remain strictly for the dog's use and is easy to keep clean.

You can start out with paper-training indoors and switch over to an outdoor surface as the puppy matures and gains control over his need to eliminate. For the naysayers, don't worry—this won't mean that the dog will soil on every piece of newspaper lying around the house. You are training him to go outside, remember? Starting out by paper-training often is the only choice for a city dog.

The first step in any kind of training, whether house-training or basic commands, is acclimating the pup to his collar and lead.

CANINE DEVELOPMENT SCHEDULE

It is important to understand how and at what age a puppy develops into adulthood. If you are a puppy owner, consult this Canine Development Schedule to determine the stage of development your puppy is currently experiencing. This knowledge will help you as you work with the puppy in the weeks and months ahead.

PERIOD	AGE	CHARACTERISTICS
FIRST TO THIRD	BIRTH TO SEVEN WEEKS	Puppy needs food, sleep and warmth and responds to simple and gentle touching. Needs mother for security and disciplining. Needs littermates for learning and interacting with other dogs. Pup learns to function within a pack and learns pack order of dominance. Begin socializing pup with adults and children for short periods. Pup begins to become aware of his environment.
FOURTH	EIGHT TO TWELVE WEEKS	Brain is fully developed. Pup needs socializing with outside world. Remove from mother and littermates. Needs to change from canine pack to human pack. Human dominance necessary. Fear period occurs between 8 and 12 weeks. Avoid fright and pain.
FIFTH	THIRTEEN TO SIXTEEN WEEKS	Training and formal obedience should begin. Less association with other dogs, more with people, places, situations. Period will pass easily if you remember this is pup's change-to-adolescence time. Be firm and fair. Flight instinct prominent. Permissiveness and over-disciplining can do permanent damage. Praise for good behavior.
JUVENILE	FOUR TO EIGHT MONTHS	Another fear period about seven to eight months of age. It passes quickly, but be cautious of fright and pain. Sexual maturity reached. Dominant traits established. Dog should understand sit, down, come and stay by now.

NOTE: THESE ARE APPROXIMATE TIME FRAMES. ALLOW FOR INDIVIDUAL DIFFERENCES IN PUPPIES.

day, plan to hire a dog-sitter or ask a neighbor to come over to take the pup outside, feed him his lunch and then take him out again about ten or so minutes after he's eaten. Also make arrangements with that or another person to be your "emergency" contact if you have to stay late on the job. Remind yourself—repeatedly—that this hectic schedule improves as the puppy gets older.

HOME WITHIN A HOME
Your Spinone puppy needs to be confined to one secure, puppy-proof area when no one is able to watch his every move. Generally the kitchen is the place of choice because the floor is washable. Likewise, it's a busy family area that will accustom the pup to a variety of noises, everything from pots and pans to the telephone, blender and dishwasher. He will also be

For the safety of your Spinoni, make sure your yard is securely fenced.

WHEN YOUR PUPPY'S "GOT TO GO"
Your puppy's need to relieve himself is seemingly non-stop, but signs of improvement will be seen each week. From 8 to 10 weeks old, the puppy will have to be taken outside every time he wakes up, about 10–15 minutes after every meal and after every period of play—all day long, from first thing in the morning until his bedtime! That's a total of ten or more trips per day to teach the puppy where it's okay to relieve himself. With that schedule in mind, you can see that house-training a young puppy is not a part-time job. It requires someone to be home all day.

If that seems overwhelming or impossible, do a little planning. For example, plan to pick up your puppy at the start of a vacation period. If you can't get home in the middle of the

An "ex-pen," sturdy enough that the pup can't knock it over and high enough that he can't climb out, is a helpful tool in confining your pup. This type of pen is portable and easily assembled.

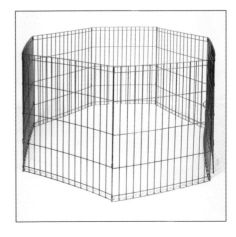

enchanted by the smell of your cooking (and will never be critical when you burn something). An exercise pen (also called an "ex-pen," a puppy version of a playpen) within the room of choice is an excellent means of confinement for a young pup. He can see out and has a certain amount of space in which to run about, but he is safe from dangerous things like electrical cords, heating units, trash baskets or open kitchen-supply cabinets. Place the pen where the puppy will not get a blast of heat or air conditioning.

In the pen, you can put a few toys, his bed (which can be his crate if the dimensions of pen and crate are compatible) and a few layers of newspaper in one small corner, just in case. A water bowl can be hung at a convenient height on the side of the ex-pen so it won't become a splashing pool for an innovative puppy. His food dish can go on the floor, next to the water bowl.

Crates are something that pet owners are at last getting used to for their dogs. Wild or domestic canines have always preferred to sleep in den-like safe spots, and that is exactly what the crate provides. How often have you seen adult dogs that choose to sleep under a table or chair even though they have full run of the house? It's the den connection.

In your "happy" voice, use the word "Crate" every time you put the pup into his den. If he's new to a crate, toss in a small

EXTRA! EXTRA!

The headlines read: "Puppy Piddles Here!" Breeders commonly use newspapers to line their whelping pens, so puppies learn to associate newspapers with relieving themselves. Do not use newspapers to line your pup's crate, as this will signal to your puppy that it is okay to urinate in his crate. If you choose to paper-train your puppy, you will layer newspapers on a section of the floor near the door he uses to go outside. You should encourage the puppy to use the papers to relieve himself, and bring him there whenever you see him getting ready to go. Little by little, you will reduce the size of the newspaper-covered area so that the puppy will learn to relieve himself "on the other side of the door."

POTTY COMMAND

Most dogs love to please their masters; there are no bounds to what dogs will do to make their owners happy. The potty command is a good example of this theory. If toileting on command makes the master happy, then more power to him. Dogs will obligingly piddle if it really makes their keepers smile. Some owners can be creative about which word they will use to command their dogs to relieve themselves. Some popular choices are "Potty," "Tinkle," "Piddle," "Let's go," "Hurry up" and "Toilet." Give the command every time your puppy goes into position and the puppy will begin to associate his business with the command.

those wake-up yips in the morning, put the crate in a corner of your bedroom. However, don't make any response whatsoever to whining or crying. If he's completely ignored, he'll settle down and get to sleep.

Good bedding for a young puppy is an old folded bath towel or an old blanket, something that is easily washable and disposable if necessary ("accidents" will happen!). Never put newspaper in the puppy's crate. Also, those old ideas about adding a clock to replace his mother's heartbeat, or a hot-water bottle to replace her warmth, are just that—old ideas. The clock could drive the puppy nuts, and the hot-water bottle could end up as a very soggy waterbed! An extremely good breeder would have introduced your puppy to the crate by letting two pups sleep together for a couple of nights, followed by several nights alone. How thankful you will be if you found that breeder!

Safe toys in the pup's crate or area will keep him occupied, but monitor their condition closely. Discard any toys that show signs of being chewed to bits. Squeaky parts, bits of stuffing or any other small pieces can cause intestinal blockage or possibly choking if swallowed.

biscuit for him to chase the first few times. At night, after he's been outside, he should sleep in his crate. The crate may be kept in his designated area at night or, if you want to be sure to hear

which is something entirely different.

Most corrections at this stage come in the form of simply

If he starts to squat indoors, scoop up your Spinone and carry him to his designated relief area...quickly!

PROGRESSING WITH POTTY-TRAINING

After you've taken your puppy out and he has relieved himself in the area you've selected, he can have some free time with the family as long as there is someone responsible for watching him. That doesn't mean just someone in the same room who is watching TV or busy on the computer, but one person who is doing nothing other than keeping an eye on the pup, playing with him on the floor and helping him understand his position in the pack.

This first taste of freedom will let you begin to set the house rules. If you don't want the dog on the furniture, now is the time to prevent his first attempts to jump up onto the couch. The word to use in this case is "Off," not "Down." "Down" is the word you will use to teach the down position,

LEASH TRAINING

House-training and leash training go hand in hand, literally. When taking your puppy outside to do his business, lead him there on his leash. Unless an emergency potty run is called for, do not whisk the puppy up into your arms and take him outside. If you have a fenced yard, you have the advantage of letting the puppy loose to go out, but it's better to put the dog on the leash and take him to his designated place in the yard until he is reliably house-trained. Taking the puppy for a walk is the best way to house-train a dog. The dog will associate the walk with his time to relieve himself, and the exercise of walking stimulates the dog's bowels and bladder. Dogs that are not trained to relieve themselves on a walk may hold it until they get back home, which of course defeats half the purpose of the walk.

DAILY SCHEDULE

How many relief trips does your puppy need per day? A puppy up to the age of 14 weeks will need to go outside about 8 to 12 times per day! You will have to take the pup out any time he starts sniffing around the floor or turning in small circles, as well as after naps, meals, games and lessons or whenever he's released from his crate. Once the puppy is 14 to 22 weeks of age, he will require only 6 to 8 relief trips. At the ages of 22 to 32 weeks, the puppy will require about 5 to 7 trips. Adult dogs typically require four relief trips per day, in the morning, afternoon, evening and late at night.

distracting the puppy. Instead of telling him "No" for "Don't chew the carpet," distract the chomping puppy with a toy and he'll forget about the carpet.

As you are playing with the pup, do not forget to watch him closely and pay attention to his body language. Whenever you see him begin to circle or sniff, take the puppy outside to relieve himself. If you are paper-training, put him back into his confined area on the newspapers. In either case, praise him as he eliminates while he actually is in the act of relieving himself. Three seconds after he has finished is too late! You'll be praising him for running toward you, picking up a toy or whatever he may be doing at that moment, and that's not what you want to be praising him for. Timing is a vital tool in all dog training. Use it.

If using newspapers, remove soiled sheets immediately and replace them with clean ones. You may want to take a small piece of soiled paper and place it in the middle of the new clean papers, as the scent will attract him to that spot when it's time to go again. That scent attraction is why it's so important to clean up any messes made in the house by using a product specially made to eliminate the odor of dog urine and droppings. Regular household cleansers won't do the trick. Pet shops sell the best pet deodorizers. Invest in the largest container you can find.

Scent attraction eventually will lead your pup to his chosen spot outdoors; this is the basis of outdoor training. When you take your puppy outside to relieve

LEADER OF THE PACK

Canines are pack animals. They live according to pack rules, and every pack has only one leader. Guess what? That's you! To establish your position of authority, lay down the rules and be fair and good-natured in all your dealings with your dog. He will consider young children as his littermates, but the one who trains him, who feeds him, who grooms him, who expects him to come into line, that's his leader. And he who leads must be obeyed.

himself, use a one-word command such as "Outside" or "Go-potty" (that's one word to the puppy!) as you pick him up and attach his leash. Then put him down in his area. If for any reason you can't carry him, snap the leash on quickly and lead him to his spot. Now comes the hard part—hard for you, that is. Just stand there until he urinates and defecates. Move him a few feet in one direction or another if he's just sitting there looking at you, but remember that this is neither playtime nor time for a walk. This is strictly a business trip! Then, as he circles and squats (remember your timing!), give him a quiet "Good dog" as praise. If you start to jump for joy, ecstatic over his perform-ance, he'll do one of two things: either he will stop mid-stream,

as it were, or he'll do it again for you—in the house—and expect you to be just as delighted!

Give him five minutes or so and, if he doesn't go in that time, take him back indoors to his confined area and try again in another ten minutes, or immediately if you see him sniffing and circling. By careful observation, you'll soon work out a successful schedule.

Accidents, by the way, are just that—accidents. Clean them up quickly and thoroughly, without comment, after the puppy has been taken outside to finish his business and then put back into his area or crate. If you witness an accident in progress, say "No!" in a stern voice and get the pup outdoors immedi-ately. No punishment is needed.

Pups can learn a lot from watching the older dogs in the "pack." Be sure, though, that the puppies know that you are the pack leader.

You and your puppy are just learning each other's language, and sometimes it's easy to miss a puppy's message. Chalk it up to experience and watch more closely from now on.

KEEPING THE PACK ORDERLY
Discipline is a form of training that brings order to life. For example, military discipline is what allows the soldiers in an army to work as one. Discipline is a form of teaching and, in dogs, is the basis of how the successful pack operates. Each member knows his place in the pack and all respect the leader, or Alpha dog. It is essential for your puppy that you establish this type of relationship, with you as the Alpha, or leader. It is a form of social coexistence that all canines recognize and accept. Discipline, therefore, is never to be confused with punishment. When you teach your puppy how you want him to behave, and he behaves properly and you praise him for it, you are disciplining him with a form of positive reinforcement.

For a dog, rewards come in the form of praise, a smile, a cheerful tone of voice, a few friendly pats or a rub of the ears. Rewards are also small food treats. Obviously, that does not mean bits of regular dog food. Instead, treats are very small bits of special things like cheese or pieces of soft dog treats. The idea is to reward the dog with something very small that he can taste and swallow, providing instant positive reinforcement. If he has to take time to chew the treat, he will have forgotten what he did to earn it by the time he is finished.

Your puppy should never be physically punished. The displeasure shown on your face and in your voice is sufficient to signal to the pup that he has done something wrong. He wants to please everyone higher up on the social ladder, especially his leader, so a scowl and harsh voice will take care of the error. Growling out the word

WHO'S TRAINING WHOM?
Dog training is a black-and-white exercise. The correct response to a command must be absolute, and the trainer must insist on completely accurate responses from the dog. A trainer cannot command his dog to sit and then settle for the dog's melting into the down position. Often owners are so pleased that their dogs "did something" in response to a command that they just shrug and say, "OK, Down" even though they wanted the dog to sit. You want your dog to respond to the command without hesitation: he must respond at that moment and correctly every time.

"Shame!" when the pup is caught in the act of doing something wrong is better than the repetitive "No." Some dogs hear "No" so often that they begin to think it's their name! By the way, do not use the dog's name when you're correcting him. His name is reserved to get his attention for something pleasant about to take place.

There are punishments that have nothing to do with you. For example, your dog may think that chasing cats is one reason for his existence. You can try to stop it as much as you like but without success, because it's such fun for the dog. But one good hissing, spitting swipe of a cat's claws across the dog's nose will put an end to the game forever. Intervene only when

your dog's eyeball is seriously at risk. Cat scratches can cause permanent damage to an innocent but annoying puppy.

PUPPY KINDERGARTEN

COLLAR AND LEASH
Before you begin your Spinone puppy's education, he must be used to his collar and leash. Choose a collar for your puppy that is secure, but not heavy or bulky. He won't enjoy training if he's uncomfortable. A flat buckle collar is fine for everyday wear and for initial puppy training. For older dogs, there are several types of training collars such as the martingale, which is a double loop that tightens slightly around the neck, or the head collar, which is similar to a horse's halter. Do not use a chain choke collar unless you have been specifically shown how to put it on and how to use

Training includes teaching and enforcing the house rules; for example, will the pup be allowed on the furniture?

BASIC PRINCIPLES OF DOG TRAINING
1. Start training early. A young puppy is ready, willing and able.
2. Timing is your all-important tool. Praise at the exact time that the dog responds correctly. Pay close attention.
3. Patience is almost as important as timing!
4. Repeat! The same word has to mean the same thing every time.
5. In the beginning, praise all correct behavior verbally, along with treats and petting.

SMILE WHEN YOU ORDER ME AROUND!

While trainers recommend practicing with your dog every day, it's perfectly acceptable to take a "mental health day" off. It's better not to train the dog on days when you're in a sour mood. Your bad attitude or lack of interest will be sensed by your dog, and he will respond accordingly. Studies show that dogs are well tuned-in to their humans' emotions. Be conscious of how you use your voice when talking to your dog. Raising your voice or shouting will only erode your dog's trust in you as his trainer and master.

it. For the Spinone, the choke collar is not the best option; owners are advised to look into other types of training collars.

A lightweight 6-foot woven cotton or nylon training leash is preferred by most trainers because it is easy to fold up in your hand and comfortable to hold because there is a certain amount of give to it. There are lessons where the dog will start off 6 feet away from you at the end of the leash. The leash used to take the puppy outside to relieve himself is shorter because you don't want him to roam away from his area. The shorter leash will also be the one to use when you walk the puppy.

If you've been wise enough to enroll in a puppy kindergarten training class, suggestions will be made as to the best collar and leash for your young puppy. I say "wise" because your puppy will be in a class with puppies in his age range (up to five months old) of all breeds and sizes. It's the perfect way for him to learn the right way (and the wrong way) to interact with other dogs as well as their people. You cannot teach your puppy how to interpret another dog's sign language. For a first-time puppy owner, these socialization classes are invaluable. For experienced dog owners, they are a real boon to further training.

ATTENTION

You've been using the dog's name since the minute you collected him from the breeder, so you should be able to get his attention by saying his name—with a big smile and in an excited tone of voice. His response will be the puppy equivalent of "Here I am! What are we going to do?" Your immediate response (if you haven't guessed by now) is "Good dog." Rewarding him at the moment he pays attention to you teaches him the proper way to respond when he hears his name.

EXERCISES FOR A BASIC CANINE EDUCATION

THE SIT EXERCISE

There are several ways to teach the puppy to sit. The first one is to catch him whenever he is about to sit and, as his backside nears the floor, say "Sit, good dog!" That's positive reinforcement and, if your timing is sharp, he will learn that what he's doing at that second is connected to your saying "Sit" and that you think he's clever for doing it!

A basic command is the sit exercise. It is simple to teach, and the dog usually learns the command quickly.

SIT AROUND THE HOUSE

"Sit" is the command you'll use most often. Your pup objects when placed in a sit with your hands, so try the "bringing the food up under his chin" method. Better still, catch him in the act! Your dog will sit on his own many times throughout the day, so let him know that he's doing the "Sit" by saying the word and rewarding him. Praise him and have him sit for everything—toys, connecting his leash, his dinner, before going out the door, etc.

Another method is to start with the puppy on his leash in front of you. Show him a treat in the palm of your right hand. Bring your hand up under his nose and, almost in slow motion, move your hand up and back so his nose goes up in the air and his head tilts back as he follows the treat in your hand. At that point, he will have to either sit or fall over, so as his back legs buckle under, say "Sit, good dog," and then give him

Training sessions should always be kept positive. Too much scolding during training is counter-productive, as the dog's trust in his master and trainer will deteriorate.

the treat and lots of praise. You may have to begin with your hand lightly running up his chest, actually lifting his chin up until he sits. Some (usually older) dogs require gentle pressure on their hindquarters with the left hand, in which case the dog should be on your left side. Puppies generally do not appreciate this physical dominance.

After a few times, you should be able to show the dog a treat in the open palm of your hand, raise your hand waist-high as you say "Sit" and have him sit. You will thereby have taught him two things at the same time. Both the verbal command and the motion of the hand are signals for the sit. Your puppy is watching you almost more than he is listening to you, so what you do is just as important as what you say.

Don't save any of these drills only for training sessions. Use them as much as possible at odd times during a normal day. The dog should always sit before being given his food dish. He should sit to let you go through a doorway first, when the doorbell rings or when you stop to speak to someone on the street.

THE DOWN EXERCISE
Before beginning to teach the down command, you must consider how the dog feels about this exercise. To him, "down" is a submissive position. Being flat on the floor with you standing

over him is not his idea of fun. It's up to you to let him know that, while it may not be fun, the reward of your approval is worth his effort.

Start with the puppy on your left side in a sit position. Hold the leash right above his collar in your left hand. Have an extra-special treat, such as a small piece of cooked chicken or hot dog, in your right hand. Place it at the end of the pup's nose and steadily move your hand down and forward along the ground. Hold the leash to prevent a sudden lunge for the food. As the puppy goes into the down position, say "Down" gently.

"SCHOOL" MODE
When is your puppy ready for a lesson? Maybe not always when you are. Attempting training with treats just before his mealtime is asking for disaster. Notice what times of day he performs best and make that Fido's school time.

The difficulty with this exercise is twofold: it's both the submissive aspect and the fact that most people say the word "Down" as if they were drill sergeants in charge of recruits! So issue the command sweetly, give him the treat and have the pup maintain the down position for several seconds. If he tries to get up immediately, place your hands on his shoulders and press down gently, giving him a very quiet "Good dog." As you progress with this lesson, increase the "down time" until he will hold it until you say "Okay" (his cue for release). Practice this one in the house at various times throughout the day.

By increasing the length of time during which the dog must maintain the down position, you'll find many uses for it. For example, he can lie at your feet in the veterinarian's office or anywhere that both of you have to wait, when you are on the

Once the dog has mastered both the down and the stay, you can practice the down/stay command without the lead in a safe area.

TRAINING WITHOUT FOOD

Some dogs (not many!) will respond easily to training if you just smile at them, adding an occasional "Good dog." Positive reinforcement based on praise can replace treats only if done correctly. All correct responses are verbally praised, with a pat on the dog's side. Incorrect responses are ignored and the exercise repeated.

phone, while the family is eating and so forth. If you progress to training for competitive obedience, he'll already be all set for the exercise called the "long down."

THE STAY EXERCISE

You can teach your Spinone to stay in the sit, down and stand positions. To teach the sit/stay, have the dog sit on your left side. Hold the leash at waist level in your left hand and let the dog know that you have a treat in your closed right hand. Step forward on your right foot as you say "Stay." Immediately turn and stand directly in front of the dog, keeping your right hand up high so he'll keep his eye on the treat hand and maintain the sit position for a count of five. Return to your original position and offer the reward.

Increase the length of the sit/stay each time until the dog can hold it for at least 30 seconds without moving. After about a week of success, move out on your right foot and take two steps before turning to face the dog. Give the "Stay" hand signal (left palm up, facing the dog) as you leave. He gets the treat when you return and he holds the sit/stay. Increase the distance that you walk away from him before turning until you reach the length of your training leash. But don't rush it! Go back to the beginning if he moves before he should. No matter what the lesson, never be upset by having to back up for a few days. The repetition and practice are what will make your dog reliable in these commands. It won't do any good to move on to something more difficult if the command is not mastered at the easier levels. Above all, even if you do get frustrated, never let your puppy know! Always keep a positive, upbeat attitude during training, which will transmit to your dog for positive results.

The down/stay is taught in the same way once the dog is completely reliable and steady with the down command. Again, don't rush it. With the dog in the down position on your left side, step out on your right foot as you say "Stay." Return by walking around in back of the dog and into your original position. While you are training, it's okay to murmur something like "Hold on" to encourage him to stay put. When the dog will stay without moving when you are at a distance of 3 or 4 feet, begin to increase the length of time before you return. Be sure he holds the down on your return until you say "Okay." At that point, he gets his treat—just so he'll remember for next time that it's not over until it's over.

THE COME EXERCISE

No command is more important to the safety of your Spinone than "Come." It is what you should say every single time you see the puppy running toward you: "Divo, come! Good dog." During playtime, run a few feet away from the puppy and turn and tell him to "Come" as he is already running to you. You can

With treats in hand, this trainer has no problem keeping the trainee's undivided attention during the sit/stay exercise.

Once your Spinone is familiar with the basic commands, you can begin using hand signals and even layer in whistle commands.

go so far as to teach your puppy two things at once if you squat down and hold out your arms. As the pup gets close to you and you're saying "Good dog," bring your right arm in about waist high. Now he's also learning the hand signal, an excellent device should you be on the phone when you need to get him to come to you! You'll also both be one step ahead when you enter obedience classes.

When the puppy responds to your well-timed "Come," try it with the puppy on the training leash. This time, catch him off guard, while he's sniffing a leaf or watching a bird: "Divo, come!" You may have to pause for a split second after his name to be sure you have his attention. If the puppy shows any sign of confusion, give the leash a mild jerk and take a couple of steps backward. Do

not repeat the command. In this case, you should say "Good come" as he reaches you.

That's the number-one rule of training. Each command word is given just once. Anything more is nagging. You'll also notice that all commands are one word only. Even when they are actually two words, you say them as one.

Never call the dog to come to you—with or without his name—if you are angry or intend to correct him for some misbehavior. When correcting the pup, you go to him. Your dog must always connect "Come" with something pleasant and with your approval; then you can rely on his response.

Puppies, like children, have notoriously short attention spans, so don't overdo it with any of the training. Keep each lesson short. Break it up with a

FROM HEEL TO ETERNITY

To begin, step away from the dog, who is in the sit position, on your right foot. That tells the dog you aren't going anywhere. Turn and stand directly in front of him so he won't be tempted to follow. Two seconds is a long, long time to your dog, so increase the time for which he's expected to stay only in short increments. Don't force it. When practicing the heel exercise, your dog will sit at your side whenever you stop. Don't stop for more than three seconds, as your enthusiastic dog will really feel that it's an eternity!

walking your growing puppy, you need to be in control. Besides, it looks terrible to be pulled and yanked down the street, and it's not much fun either. Your eight- to ten-week-old puppy will probably follow you everywhere, but that's his natural instinct, not your control over the situation. However, any time he does follow you, you can say "Heel" and be ahead of the game, as he will learn to associate this command with the action of following you before you even begin teaching him to heel.

quick run around the yard or a ball toss, repeat the lesson and quit as soon as the pup gets it right. That way, you will always end with a "Good dog."

Life isn't perfect and neither are puppies. A time will come, often around ten months of age, when he'll become "selectively deaf" or choose to "forget" his name. He may respond by wagging his tail (and even seeming to smile at you) with a look that says "Make me!" Laugh, throw his favorite toy and skip the lesson you had planned. Pups will be pups!

The Heel Exercise

The second most important command to teach, after the come, is the heel. When you are

A Spinone heels in the show ring as his gait is evaluated. Learning to heel is necessary for all dogs, not just show dogs.

BE UPSTANDING!
You are the dog's leader. During training, stand up straight so your dog looks up at you, and therefore up *to* you. Say the command words distinctly, in a clear, declarative tone of voice. (No jumping!) Give rewards only as the correct response takes place (remember your timing!). Praise, smiles and treats are "rewards" used to positively reinforce correct responses. Don't repeat a mistake. Just change to another exercise—you will soon find success!

There is a very precise, almost military, procedure for teaching your dog to heel. As with all other obedience training, begin with the dog on your left side. He will be in a very nice sit and you will have the training leash across your chest. Hold the loop and folded leash in your right hand. Pick up the slack leash above the dog in your left hand and hold it loosely at your side. Step out on your left foot as you say "Heel." If the puppy does not move, give a gentle tug or pat your left leg to get him started. If he surges ahead of you, stop and pull him back gently until he is at your side. Tell him to sit and begin again.

Walk a few steps and stop while the puppy is correctly beside you. Tell him to sit and give mild verbal praise. (More enthusiastic praise will encourage him to think the lesson is over.) Repeat the lesson, increasing the number of steps you take only as long as the dog is heeling nicely beside you. When you end the lesson, have him hold the sit, then give him the "Okay" to let him know that this is the end of the lesson. Praise him so that he knows he did a good job.

The cure for excessive pulling (a common problem) is to stop when the dog is no more than 2 or 3 feet ahead of you.

Guide him back into position and begin again. With a really determined puller, try switching to a head collar. This will automatically turn the pup's head toward you so you can bring him back easily to the heel position. Give quiet, reassuring praise every time the leash goes slack and he's staying with you.

Staying and heeling can take a lot out of a dog, so provide playtime and free-running exercise to shake off the stress when the lessons are over. You don't want him to associate training with all work and no fun.

TAPERING OFF TIDBITS

Your dog has been watching you—and the hand that treats—throughout all of his lessons, and now it's time to break the treat habit. Begin by giving him treats at the end of each lesson only. Then start to give a treat after the end of only some of the lessons. At the end of every lesson, as well as during the lessons, be consistent with the praise. Your pup now doesn't know whether he'll get a treat or not, but he should keep performing well just in case! Finally, you will stop giving treat rewards entirely. Save them for something brand-new that you want to teach him. Keep up the praise and you'll always have a "good dog."

OBEDIENCE CLASSES

The advantages of an obedience class are that your dog will have to learn amid the distractions of other people and dogs and that your mistakes will be quickly corrected by the trainer. Teaching

NO MORE TREATS!

When your dog is responding promptly and correctly to commands, it's time to eliminate treats. Begin by alternating a treat reward with a verbal-praise-only reward. Gradually eliminate all treats while increasing the frequency of praise. Overlook pleading eyes and expectant expressions, but if he's still watching your treat hand, you're on your way to using hand signals.

Your puppy's first training instructor was his dam, but now it is your turn to take over the role as teacher and nurturer.

your dog along with a qualified instructor and other handlers who may have more dog experience than you is another plus of the class environment. The instructor and other handlers can help you to find the most efficient way of teaching your dog a command or exercise. It's often easier to learn from other people's mistakes than your own. You will also learn all of the requirements for competitive obedience trials, in which you can earn titles and go on to advanced jumping and retrieving exercises, which are fun for many dogs. Obedience classes build the foundation needed for many other canine activities (in which we humans are allowed to participate, too!).

HOW DO I GET TO CARNEGIE HALL?

Or the National Obedience Championships? The same way you get your dog to do anything else—practice, practice, practice. It's *how* you practice that counts. Keep sessions positive, short, varied, interesting and interspersed with active fun. A bored dog isn't learning. If you're feeling out of sorts yourself, quit for the day. Set yourself a reasonable schedule for several brief practice sessions every day and stick to it. Practice randomly throughout the day as you're doing different things around the house. Lots of praise for that good "Sit" in front of the TV or while waiting for his dinner!

Playtime can happen both indoors and out. A young puppy is growing so rapidly that he needs sleep more than he needs a lot of physical exercise. Puppies get sufficient exercise on their own just through normal puppy activity. Monitor play with young children so you can remove the puppy when he's had enough, or calm the kids if they get too rowdy. Almost all puppies love to chase after a toy you've thrown, and you can turn your games into educational activities. Every time your puppy brings the toy back to you, say "Give it" (or "Drop it") followed by "Good dog" and throwing it again. If he's reluctant to give it to you, offer a small treat so that he drops the toy as he takes the treat. He will soon get the idea.

OTHER ACTIVITIES FOR LIFE

Whether a dog is trained in the structured environment of a class or alone with his owner at home, there are many activities that can bring fun and rewards to both owner and dog once they have mastered basic control.

Teaching the dog to help out around the home, in the garden or on the farm provides great satisfaction to both dog and owner. In addition, the dog's help makes life a little easier for his owner and raises his stature as a valued companion to his family. It helps give the dog a purpose by occupying his mind and providing an outlet for his energy.

Backpacking is an exciting and healthy activity that the dog can be taught without assistance from more than his owner. The exercise of walking and climbing is good for man and dog alike, and the bond that they develop together is priceless. The rule for backpacking with any dog is never to expect the dog to carry more than one-sixth of his body weight.

If you are interested in participating in organized competition with your Spinone, there are activities other than obedience in which you and your dog can become involved. The most obvious of these for the Spinone owner are field trials, organized outings that test the breed's natural hunting ability. Field trials are not

Early socialization with your other household pets will result in a pleasant, biddable pup.

designed for the casual partici-
pant, as the sport requires significant investment of time, talent,
effort and money. Hunting tests
are more informal and good for
those owners who want to
develop their dogs' instincts but
do not want to commit to the
demands of field-trial training and
competition. You can find out
more about field and hunting
events by contacting the AKC or
the Spinone Italiano Club of
America.

Agility is a popular sport in
which dogs run through an
obstacle course that includes
various jumps, tunnels and other
exercises to test the dog's speed
and coordination. The owners run
beside their dogs to give

Retriever training in progress! Spinoni love activities that utilize their natural abilities and energy.

> ### TIPS FOR
> ### TRAINING AND SAFETY
> 1. Whether on or off leash, practice only in a fenced area.
> 2. Remove the training collar when the training session is over.
> 3. Don't try to break up a dogfight.
> 4. "Come," "Leave it" and "Wait" are safety commands.
> 5. The dog belongs in a crate or behind a barrier when riding in the car.
> 6. Don't ignore the dog's first sign of aggression. Aggression only gets worse, so take it seriously.
> 7. Keep the faces of children and dogs separated.
> 8. Pay attention to what the dog is chewing.
> 9. Keep the vet's number near your phone.
> 10. "Okay" is a useful release command.

commands and to guide them
through the course. Although
competitive, the focus is on fun—
it's fun to do, fun to watch and
great exercise.

Whatever activities and sports
you decide to undertake with
your Spinone, you will certainly
be glad that you invested the time
to train him properly. From the
basics of obedience to the rigorous
education of competitive trials,
the Spinone is a gifted student
who wants nothing more than to
delight his master.

The water retrieve:
TOP: The Spinone
swims out to the
bird, which has
been shot over
the water.
BOTTOM: The
Spinone holds the
bird gently in his
mouth while
returning to shore.

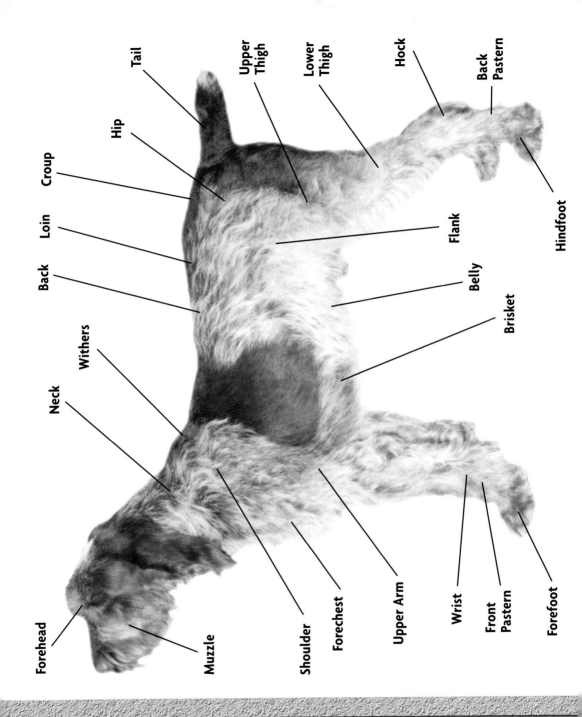

Forehead

Neck

Withers

Back

Loin

Croup

Hip

Tail

Upper Thigh

Lower Thigh

Hock

Back Pastern

Hindfoot

Flank

Belly

Brisket

Muzzle

Shoulder

Forechest

Upper Arm

Wrist

Front Pastern

Forefoot

PHYSICAL STRUCTURE OF THE SPINONE ITALIANO

HEALTHCARE OF YOUR

SPINONE ITALIANO

By Lowell Ackerman DVM, DACVD

HEALTHCARE FOR A LIFETIME

When you own a dog, you become his healthcare advocate over his entire lifespan, as well as being the one to shoulder the financial burden of such care. Accordingly, it is worthwhile to focus on prevention rather than treatment, as you and your pet will both be happier.

Of course, the best place to have begun your program of preventive healthcare is with the initial purchase or adoption of your dog. There is no way of guaranteeing that your new furry friend is free of medical problems, but there are some things you can do to improve your odds. You certainly should have done adequate research into the Spinone and have selected your puppy carefully rather than buying on impulse. Health issues aside, a large number of pet abandonment and relinquishment cases arise from a mismatch between pet needs and owner expectations. This is entirely preventable with appropriate planning and finding a good breeder.

Regarding healthcare issues specifically, it is very difficult to make blanket statements about where to acquire a problem-free pet, but, again, a reputable breeder is your best bet. In an ideal situation you have the opportunity to see both parents, get references from other owners of the breeder's pups and see genetic-testing documentation for several generations of the litter's ancestors. At the very least, you must thoroughly investigate your breed of interest and the problems inherent in that breed, as well as the genetic testing available to screen for those problems. Genetic testing offers some important benefits, but testing is available for only a few disorders in a relatively small number of breeds and is not available for some of the most common genetic diseases, such as hip dysplasia, cataracts, epilepsy, cardiomyopathy, etc. This area of research is indeed exciting and increasingly important, and advances will continue to be made each year. In fact, recent research has shown that there is an equivalent dog gene for 75% of known human genes, so research done in either species is likely to benefit the other.

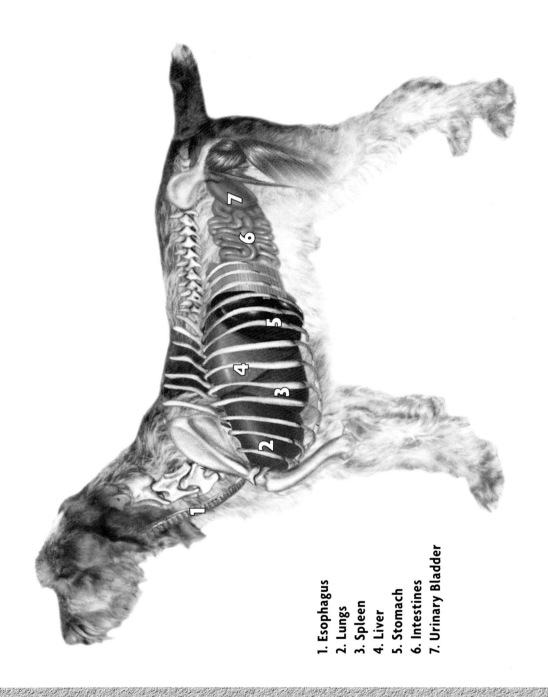

1. Esophagus
2. Lungs
3. Spleen
4. Liver
5. Stomach
6. Intestines
7. Urinary Bladder

INTERNAL ORGANS OF THE SPINONE ITALIANO

We've also discussed that evaluating the behavioral nature of your Spinone and that of his immediate family members is an important part of the selection process that cannot be underestimated or overemphasized. It is sometimes difficult to evaluate temperament in puppies because certain behavioral tendencies, such as some forms of aggression, may not be immediately evident. More dogs are euthanized each year for behavioral reasons than for all medical conditions combined, so it is critical to take temperament issues seriously. Start with a well-balanced, friendly companion and put the time and effort into proper socialization, and you will both be rewarded with a longtime valued relationship.

Assuming that you have started off with a pup from healthy, sound stock, you then become responsible for helping your veterinarian keep your pet healthy. Some crucial things happen before you even bring your puppy home. Parasite control typically begins at two weeks of age, and vaccinations typically begin at six to eight weeks of age. A pre-pubertal evaluation is typically scheduled for about six months of age. At this time, a dental evaluation is done (since the adult teeth are now in), heartworm prevention is started and neutering or spaying is most commonly done.

DENTAL WARNING SIGNS

A veterinary dental exam is necessary if you notice one or any combination of the following in your dog:
- Broken, loose or missing teeth
- Loss of appetite (which could be due to mouth pain or illness caused by infection)
- Gum abnormalities, including redness, swelling and bleeding
- Drooling, with or without blood
- Yellowing of the teeth or gumline, indicating tartar
- Bad breath

It is critical to commence regular dental care at home if you have not already done so. It may not sound very important, but most dogs have active periodontal disease by four years of age if they don't have their teeth cleaned regularly at home, not just at their veterinary exams. Dental problems lead to more than just bad "doggy breath." Gum disease can have very serious medical consequences. If you start brushing your dog's teeth and using antiseptic rinses from a young age, your dog will be accustomed to it and will not resist. The results will be healthy dentition, which your pet will need to enjoy a long, healthy life.

Most dogs are considered adults at a year of age, although some larger breeds still have some filling out to do up to about two or

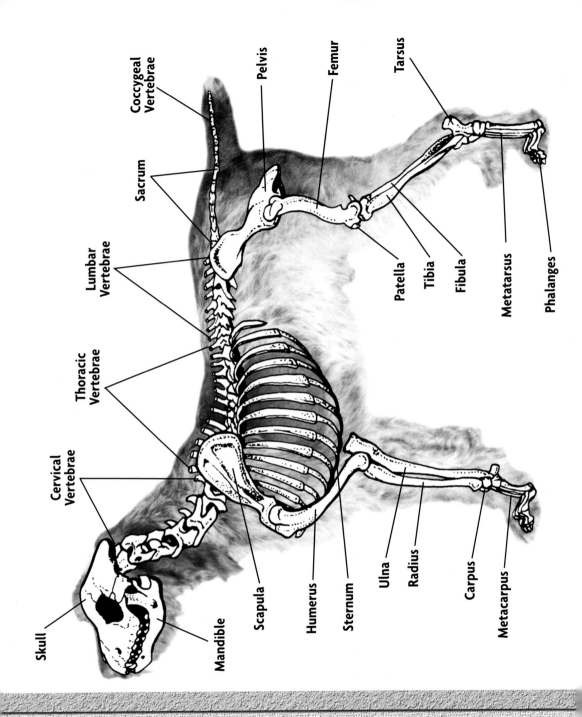

Coccygeal Vertebrae

Pelvis

Femur

Tarsus

Sacrum

Patella

Tibia

Fibula

Metatarsus

Phalanges

Lumbar Vertebrae

Thoracic Vertebrae

Cervical Vertebrae

Skull

Mandible

Scapula

Humerus

Sternum

Ulna

Radius

Carpus

Metacarpus

SKELETAL STRUCTURE OF THE SPINONE ITALIANO

so years old. Even individual dogs within each breed have different healthcare requirements, so work with your veterinarian to determine what will be needed and what your role should be. This doctor-client relationship is important, because as vaccination guidelines change, there may not be an annual "vaccine visit" scheduled. You must make sure that you see your veterinarian at least annually, even if no vaccines are due, because this is the best opportunity to coordinate health-care activities and to make sure that no medical issues creep by unaddressed.

When your Spinone reaches three-quarters of his anticipated lifespan, he is considered a "senior" and likely requires some special care. In general, if you've been taking great care of your canine companion throughout his formative and adult years, the transition to senior status should be a smooth one. Age is not a disease, and as long as everything is functioning as it should, there is no reason why most of late adulthood should not be rewarding for both you and your pet. This is especially true if you have tended to the details, such as regular veterinary visits, proper dental care, excellent nutrition and management of bone and joint issues.

At this stage in your Spinone's life, your veterinarian may want to

TAKING YOUR DOG'S TEMPERATURE

It is important to know how to take your dog's temperature at times when you think he may be ill. It's not the most enjoyable task, but it can be done without too much difficulty. It's easier with a helper, preferably someone with whom the dog is friendly, so that one of you can hold the dog while the other inserts the thermometer.

Before inserting the thermometer, coat the end with petroleum jelly. Insert the thermometer slowly and gently into the dog's rectum about one inch. Wait for the reading, about two minutes. Be sure to remove the thermometer carefully and clean it thoroughly after each use.

A dog's normal body temperature is between 100.5 and 102.5 degrees F. Immediate veterinary attention is required if the dog's temperature is below 99 or above 104 degrees F.

schedule visits twice yearly, instead of once, to run some laboratory screenings, electrocardiograms and the like, and to change the diet to something more digestible. Catching problems early is the best way to manage them effectively. Treating the early stages of heart disease is so much easier than trying to intervene when there is more significant damage to the heart muscle. Similarly, managing the beginning

INSURANCE FOR YOUR PET
Pet insurance policies are very cost-effective (and very inexpensive by human health-insurance standards), but make sure that you buy the policy long before you intend to use it (preferably starting in puppyhood, because coverage will exclude pre-existing conditions) and that you are actually buying an indemnity insurance plan from an insurance company that is regulated by your state or province. Many insurance policy look-alikes are actually discount clubs that are redeemable only at specific locations and for specific services. An indemnity plan covers your pet at almost all veterinary, specialty and emergency practices and is an excellent way to manage your pet's ongoing health-care needs.

of kidney problems is fairly routine if there is no significant kidney damage. Other problems, like cognitive dysfunction (similar to senility and Alzheimer's disease), cancer, diabetes and arthritis, are more common in older dogs, but all can be treated to help the dog live as many happy, comfortable years as possible. Just as in people, medical management is more effective (and less expensive) when you catch things early.

SELECTING A VETERINARIAN
There is probably no more important decision that you will make regarding your pet's health-care than the selection of his doctor. Your pet's veterinarian will be a pediatrician, family-practice physician and gerontologist, depending on the dog's life stage, and will be the individual who makes recommendations regarding issues such as when specialists need to be consulted, when diagnostic testing and/or therapeutic intervention is needed and when you will need to seek outside emergency and critical-care services. Your vet will act as your advocate and liaison throughout these processes.

Everyone has his own idea about what to look for in a vet, an individual who will play a big role in his dog's (and, of course, his own) life for many years to come. For some, it is the compassionate caregiver with whom they hope to develop a professional relationship to span the lifetime of their dogs and even their future pets. For others, they are seeking a clinician with keen diagnostic and therapeutic insight who can deliver state-of-the-art healthcare. Still others need a veterinary facility that is open evenings and weekends, is in close proximity or provides mobile veterinary services to accommodate their schedules; these people may not much mind that their dogs might see different veterinarians on each visit. Just as we have different reasons for selecting our own healthcare professionals (e.g., covered by insurance plan, expert in field, convenient location, etc.), we should not expect that there is a one-size-fits-all recommendation for selecting a veterinarian and veterinary practice. The best advice is to be honest in your assessment of what you expect from a veterinary practice and to conscientiously research the options in your area. You will quickly appreciate that not all veterinary practices are the same, and you will be happiest with one that truly meets your needs.

There is another point to be considered in the selection of veterinary services. Not that long ago, a single veterinarian would attempt to manage all medical and surgical issues as they arose. That was often problematic, because veterinarians are trained in many species and many diseases, and it was just impossible for general veterinary practitioners to be experts in every species, every breed, every field and every ailment. However, just as in the human healthcare fields, specialization has allowed general practitioners to concentrate on primary healthcare delivery, especially wellness and the prevention of

These two healthy and alert Spinoni are ready for some field action. A very important aspect of maintaining a healthy, active dog is the selection of a qualified veterinarian.

COMMON INFECTIOUS DISEASES

Let's discuss some of the diseases that create the need for vaccination in the first place. Following are the major canine infectious diseases and a simple explanation of each.

Rabies: A devastating viral disease that can be fatal in dogs and people. In fact, vaccination of dogs and cats is an important public-health measure to create a resistant animal buffer population to protect people from contracting the disease. Vaccination schedules are determined on a government level and are not optional for pet owners; rabies vaccination is required by law in all 50 states.

Parvovirus: A severe, potentially life-threatening disease that is easily transmitted between dogs. There are four strains of the virus, but it is believed that there is significant "cross-protection" between strains that may be included in individual vaccines.

Distemper: A potentially severe and life-threatening disease with a relatively high risk of exposure, especially in certain regions. In very high-risk distemper environments, young pups may be vaccinated with human measles vaccine, a related virus that offers cross-protection when administered at four to ten weeks of age.

Hepatitis: Caused by canine adenovirus type 1 (CAV-1), but since vaccination with the causative virus has a higher rate of adverse effects, cross-protection is derived from the use of adenovirus type 2 (CAV-2), a cause of respiratory disease and one of the potential causes of canine cough. Vaccination with CAV-2 provides long-term immunity against hepatitis, but relatively less protection against respiratory infection.

Canine cough: Also called tracheobronchitis, actually a fairly complicated result of viral and bacterial offenders; therefore, even with vaccination, protection is incomplete. Wherever dogs congregate, canine cough will likely be spread among them. Intranasal vaccination with *Bordetella* and parainfluenza is the best safeguard, but the duration of immunity does not appear to be very long, typically a year at most. These are non-core vaccines, but vaccination is sometimes mandated by boarding kennels, obedience classes, dog shows and other places where dogs congregate to try to minimize spread of infection.

Leptospirosis: A potentially fatal disease that is more common in some geographic regions. It is capable of being spread to humans. The disease varies with the individual "serovar," or strain, of *Leptospira* involved. Since there does not appear to be much cross-protection between serovars, protection is only as good as the likelihood that the serovar in the vaccine is the same as the one in the pet's local environment. Problems with *Leptospira* vaccines are that protection does not last very long, side effects are not uncommon and a large percentage of dogs (perhaps 30%) may not respond to vaccination.

Borrelia burgdorferi: The cause of Lyme disease, the risk of which varies with the geographic area in which the pet lives and travels. Lyme disease is spread by deer ticks in the eastern US and western black-legged ticks in the western part of the country, and the risk of exposure is high in some regions. Lameness, fever and inappetence are most commonly seen in affected dogs. The extent of protection from the vaccine has not been conclusively demonstrated.

Coronavirus: This disease has a high risk of exposure, especially in areas where dogs congregate, but it typically causes only mild to moderate digestive upset (diarrhea, vomiting, etc.). Vaccines are available, but the duration of protection is believed to be relatively short and the effectiveness of the vaccine in preventing infection is considered low.

There are many other vaccinations available, including those for *Giardia* and canine adenovirus-1. While there may be some specific indications for their use, and local risk factors to be considered, they are not widely recommended for most dogs.

infectious diseases, and to utilize a network of specialists to assist in the management of conditions that require specific expertise and experience. Thus there are now many types of veterinary specialists, including dermatologists, cardiologists, ophthalmologists, surgeons, internists, oncologists, neurologists, behaviorists, criticalists and others to help primary-care veterinarians deal with complicated medical challenges. In most cases, specialists see cases referred by primary-care veterinarians, make diagnoses and set up management plans. From there, the animals' ongoing care is returned to their primary-care veterinarians. This important team approach to your pet's medical-care needs has provided opportunities for advanced care and an unparalleled level of quality to be delivered.

With all of the opportunities for your Spinone to receive high-quality veterinary medical care, there is another topic that needs to be addressed at the same time—cost. It's been said that you can have excellent healthcare or inexpensive healthcare but never both; this is as true in veterinary medicine as it is in human medicine. While veterinary costs are a fraction of what the same services cost in the human healthcare arena, it is still difficult to deal with unanticipated medical costs, especially since they can easily creep into hundreds or even

thousands of dollars if specialists or emergency services become involved. However, there are ways of managing these risks. The easiest is to buy pet health insurance and realize that its foremost purpose is not to cover routine healthcare visits but rather to serve as an umbrella for those rainy days when your pet needs medical care and you don't want to worry about whether or not you can afford that care.

VACCINATIONS AND INFECTIOUS DISEASES

There has never been an easier time to prevent a variety of infectious diseases in your dog, but the advances we've made in veterinary medicine come with a price—choice. Now while it may seem that choice is a good thing (and it is), it has never been more difficult for the pet owner (or the veterinarian) to make an informed decision about the best way to protect pets through vaccination.

Years ago, it was just accepted that puppies got a starter series of vaccinations and then annual "boosters" throughout their lives to keep them protected. As more and more vaccines became available, consumers wanted the convenience of having all of that protection in a single injection. The result was "multivalent" vaccines that crammed a lot of protection into a single syringe. The manufacturers' recommendations were to give the vaccines annually, and this was a simple enough protocol to follow. However, as veterinary medicine has become more sophisticated and we have started looking more at healthcare quandaries rather than convenience, it became necessary to reevaluate the situation and deal with some tough questions. It is important to realize that whether or not to use a particular vaccine depends on the risk of contracting the disease against which it protects, the severity of the disease if it is contracted, the duration of immunity provided by the vaccine, the safety of the product and the needs of the individual animal. In a very general sense, rabies, distemper, hepatitis and parvovirus are considered core vaccine needs, while parainfluenza, *Bordetella bronchiseptica*, leptospirosis, coronavirus and borreliosis (Lyme disease) are considered non-core needs and best reserved for animals that demonstrate reasonable risk of contracting the diseases.

NEUTERING/SPAYING
Sterilization procedures (neutering for males/spaying for females) are meant to accomplish several purposes. While the underlying premise is to address the risk of pet overpopulation, there are some medical and behavioral benefits to the surgeries as well. For females, spaying prior to the first estrus (heat cycle) leads to a marked reduction in the risk of mammary

cancer. There also will be no manifestations of "heat" to attract male dogs and no bleeding in the house. For males, there is prevention of testicular cancer and a reduction in the risk of prostate problems. In both sexes there may be some limited reduction in aggressive behaviors toward other dogs, and some diminishing of urine marking, roaming and mounting.

While neutering and spaying do indeed prevent animals from contributing to pet overpopulation, even no-cost and low-cost neutering options have not eliminated the problem. Perhaps one of the main reasons for this is that individuals that intentionally breed their dogs and those that allow their animals to run at large are the main causes of unwanted offspring. Also, animals in shelters are often there because they were abandoned or relinquished, not because they came from unplanned matings. Neutering/spaying is important, but it should be considered in the context of the real causes of animals' ending up in shelters and eventually being euthanized.

One of the important considerations regarding neutering is that it is a surgical procedure. This sometimes gets lost in discussions of low-cost procedures and commoditization of the process. In females, spaying is specifically referred to as an ovariohyster-

SPAY'S THE WAY

Although spaying a female dog qualifies as major surgery—an ovariohysterectomy, in fact—this procedure is regarded as routine when performed by a qualified veterinarian on a healthy dog. The advantages to spaying a bitch are many and great. Spayed dogs do not develop uterine cancer or any life-threatening diseases of the genitals. Likewise, spayed dogs are at a significantly reduced risk of breast cancer. Bitches (and owners) are relieved of the demands of heat cycles. A spayed bitch will not leave bloody stains on your furniture during estrus, and you will not have to contend with single-minded macho males trying to climb your fence in order to seduce her. The spayed bitch's coat will not show the ill effects of her estrogen level's climbing such as a dull, lackluster outer coat or patches of hairlessness.

ectomy. In this procedure, a midline incision is made in the abdomen and the entire uterus and both ovaries are surgically removed. While this is a major invasive surgical procedure, it usually has few complications because it is typically performed on healthy young animals. However, it is major surgery, as any woman who has had a hysterectomy will attest.

In males, neutering has traditionally referred to castration, which involves the surgical removal of both testicles. While still a significant piece of surgery, there is not the abdominal exposure that is required in the female surgery. In addition, there is now a chemical sterilization option, in which a solution is injected into each testicle, leading to atrophy of the sperm-producing cells. This can typically be done under sedation rather than full anesthesia. This is a relatively new approach, and there are no long-term clinical studies yet available.

Neutering/spaying is typically done around six months of age at most veterinary hospitals, although techniques have been pioneered to perform the procedures in animals as young as eight weeks of age. In general, the surgeries on the very young animals are done for the specific reason of sterilizing them before they go to their new homes. This is done in some shelter hospitals for assurance that the animals will definitely not produce any pups. Otherwise, these organizations need to rely on owners to comply with their wishes to have the animals "altered" at a later date, something that does not always happen.

There are some exciting immunocontraceptive "vaccines" currently under development, and there may be a time when contraception in pets will not require surgical procedures. We anxiously await these developments.

A scanning electron micrograph of a dog flea, *Ctenocephalides canis*, on dog hair.

EXTERNAL PARASITES

FLEAS

Fleas have been around for millions of years and, while we have better tools now for controlling them than at any time in the past, there still is little chance that they will end up on an endangered species list. Actually, they are very well adapted to living on our pets, and they continue to adapt as we make advances.

The female flea can consume 15 times her weight in blood during active reproduction and can lay as many as 40 eggs a day. These eggs are very resistant to the effects of insecticides. They hatch into larvae, which then mature and spin cocoons. The immature fleas reside in this pupal stage until the time is right for feeding. This pupal stage is also very resistant to the effects of insecticides, and pupae can last in the environment without feeding for many months. Newly emergent fleas are attracted to animals by the warmth of the animals' bodies, movement and exhaled carbon dioxide. However, when they first emerge from their cocoons, they orient towards light; thus when an animal passes between a flea and the light source, casting a shadow, the flea pounces and starts to feed. If the animal turns out to be a dog or cat, the reproductive cycle continues. If the flea lands on another type of animal, including a person, the flea will bite but will then look for a more appropriate host. An emerging adult flea can survive without feeding for up to 12 months but, once it tastes blood, it can survive off its host for only 3 to 4 days.

It was once thought that fleas spend most of their lives in the environment, but we now know that fleas won't willingly jump off a dog unless leaping to another dog or when physically removed by brushing, bathing or other manipulation. Flea eggs, on the other hand, are shiny and smooth, and they roll off the animal and into the environment. The eggs, larvae and pupae then exist in the environment, but once the adult finds a susceptible animal, it's home sweet home until the flea is forced to seek refuge elsewhere.

Since adult fleas live on the animal and immature forms survive in the environment, a successful treatment plan must address all stages of the flea life cycle. There are now several safe and effective flea-control products that can be applied on a monthly

> ### FLEA PREVENTION FOR YOUR DOG
> - Discuss with your veterinarian the safest product to protect your dog, likely in the form of a monthly tablet or a liquid preparation placed on the back of the dog's neck.
> - For dogs suffering from flea-bite dermatitis, a shampoo or topical insecticide treatment is required.
> - Your lawn and property should be sprayed with an insecticide designed to kill fleas and ticks that lurk outdoors.
> - Using a flea comb, check the dog's coat regularly for any signs of parasites.
> - Practice good housekeeping. Vacuum floors, carpets and furniture regularly, especially in the areas that the dog frequents, and wash the dog's bedding weekly.
> - Follow up house-cleaning with carpet shampoos and sprays to rid the house of fleas at all stages of development. Insect growth regulators are the safest option.

basis. These include fipronil, imidacloprid, selamectin and permethrin (found in several formulations). Most of these products have significant flea-killing rates within 24 hours. However, none of them will control the immature forms in the environment. To accomplish this, there are a variety of insect growth regulators that can be

THE FLEA'S LIFE CYCLE

What came first, the flea or the egg? This age-old mystery is more difficult to comprehend than the actual cycle of the flea. Fleas usually live only about four months. A female can lay 2,000 eggs in her lifetime.

PHOTO BY CAROLINA BIOLOGICAL SUPPLY CO.

Egg

After ten days of rolling around your carpet or under your furniture, the eggs hatch into larvae, which feed on various and sundry debris. In days or months, depending on the climate, the larvae spin cocoons and develop into the pupal or nymph stage, which quickly develop into fleas.

Larva

PHOTO BY CAROLINA BIOLOGICAL SUPPLY CO.

Pupa

These immature fleas must locate a host within 10 to 14 days or they will die. Only about 1% of the flea population exist as adult fleas, while the other 99% exist as eggs, larvae or pupae.

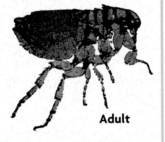

Adult

KILL FLEAS THE NATURAL WAY

If you choose not to go the route of conventional medication, there are some natural ways to ward off fleas:

- Dust your dog with a natural flea powder, composed of such herbal goodies as rosemary, wormwood, pennyroyal, citronella, rue, tobacco powder and eucalyptus.
- Apply diatomaceous earth, the fossilized remains of single-cell algae, to your carpets, furniture and pet's bedding. Even though it's not good for dogs, it's even worse for fleas, which will dry up swiftly and die.
- Brush your dog frequently, give him adequate exercise and let him fast occasionally. All of these activities strengthen the dog's immune system and make him more resistant to disease and parasites.
- Bathe your dog with a capful of pennyroyal or eucalyptus oil.
- Feed a natural diet, free of additives and preservatives. Add some fresh garlic and brewer's yeast to the dog's morning portion, as these items have flea-repelling properties.

sprayed into the environment (e.g., pyriproxyfen, methoprene, fenoxycarb) as well as insect development inhibitors such as lufenuron that can be administered. These compounds have no effect on adult fleas, but they stop immature forms from developing into adults. In years gone by, we relied heavily on toxic insecticides (such as organophosphates, organochlorines and carbamates) to manage the flea problem, but today's options are not only much safer to use on our pets but also safer for the environment.

TICKS

Ticks are members of the spider class (arachnids) and are blood-sucking parasites capable of transmitting a variety of diseases, including Lyme disease, ehrlichiosis, babesiosis and Rocky Mountain spotted fever. It's easy to see ticks on your own skin, but it is more of a challenge when your furry companion is affected. Whenever you happen to be planning a stroll in a tick-infested area (especially forests, grassy or wooded areas or parks) be prepared to do a thorough inspection of your dog afterward to search for ticks. Ticks can be tricky, so make sure you spend time looking in the ears, between the toes and everywhere else where a tick might hide. Ticks need to be attached for 24–72 hours before they transmit most of the diseases that they carry, so you do have a window of opportunity for some preventive intervention.

A TICKING BOMB

There is nothing good about a tick's harpooning his nose into your dog's skin. Among the diseases caused by ticks are Rocky Mountain spotted fever, canine ehrlichiosis, canine babesiosis, canine hepatozoonosis and Lyme disease. If a dog is allergic to the saliva of a female wood tick, he can develop tick paralysis.

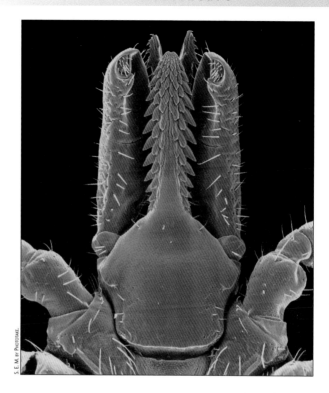

S. E. M. BY PHOTOTAKE.

Female ticks live to eat and breed. They can lay between 4,000 and 5,000 eggs and they die soon after. Males, on the other hand, live only to mate with the females and continue the process as long as they are able. Most ticks live on multiple hosts before parasitizing dogs. The immature forms typically reside on grass and shrubs, waiting for susceptible animals to walk by. The larvae and nymph stages typically feed on wildlife.

If only a few ticks are present on a dog, they can be plucked out, but it is important to remove the entire head and mouthparts,

A scanning electron micrograph of the head of a female deer tick, *Ixodes dammini,* a parasitic tick that carries Lyme disease.

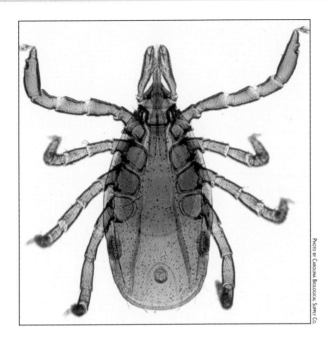

Photo by Carolina Biological Supply Co.

Deer tick,
Ixodes dammini.

which may be deeply embedded in the skin. This is best accomplished with forceps designed especially for this purpose; fingers can be used but should be protected with rubber gloves, plastic wrap or at least a paper towel. The tick should be grasped as closely as possible to the animal's skin and should be pulled upward with steady, even pressure. Do not squeeze, crush or puncture the body of the tick or you risk exposure to any disease carried by that tick. Once the ticks have been removed, the sites of attachment should be disinfected. Your hands should then be washed with soap and water to further minimize risk of contagion. The tick should be

disposed of in a container of alcohol or household bleach.

Some of the newer flea products, specifically those with fipronil, selamectin and permethrin, have effect against some, but not all, species of tick. Flea collars containing appropriate pesticides (e.g., propoxur, chlorfenvinphos) can aid in tick control. In most areas, such collars should be placed on animals in March, at the beginning of the tick season, and changed regularly. Leaving the collar on when the pesticide level is waning invites the development of resistance. Amitraz collars are also good for tick control, and the active ingredient does not interfere with other flea-control products. The ingredient helps prevent the attachment of ticks to the skin and will cause those ticks already on the skin to detach themselves.

TICK CONTROL

Removal of underbrush and leaf litter and the thinning of trees in areas where tick control is desired are recommended. These actions remove the cover and food sources for small animals that serve as hosts for ticks. With continued mowing of grasses in these areas, the probability of ticks' surviving is further reduced. A variety of insecticide ingredients (e.g., resmethrin, carbaryl, permethrin, chlorpyrifos, dioxathion and allethrin) are registered for tick control around the home.

MITES

Mites are tiny arachnid parasites that parasitize the skin of dogs. Skin diseases caused by mites are referred to as "mange," and there are many different forms seen in dogs. These forms are very different from one another, each one warranting an individual description.

Sarcoptic mange, or scabies, is one of the itchiest conditions that affects dogs. The microscopic *Sarcoptes* mites burrow into the superficial layers of the skin and can drive dogs crazy with itchiness. They are also communicable to people, although they can't complete their reproductive cycle on people. In addition to being tiny, the mites also are often difficult to find when trying to make a diagnosis. Skin scrapings from multiple areas are examined microscopically but, even then, sometimes the mites cannot be found.

Fortunately, scabies is relatively easy to treat, and there are a variety of products that will successfully kill the mites. Since the mites can't live in the environment for very long without feeding, a complete cure is usually possible within four to eight weeks.

Cheyletiellosis is caused by a relatively large mite, which sometimes can be seen even without a microscope. Often referred to as "walking dandruff," this also causes itching, but not usually as profound as with scabies.

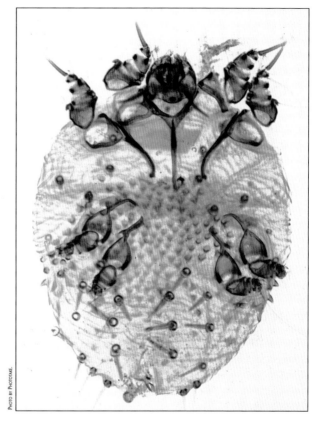

PHOTO BY PHOTOTAKE.

Sarcoptes scabiei, commonly known as the "itch mite."

While *Cheyletiella* mites can survive somewhat longer in the environment than scabies mites, they too are relatively easy to treat, being responsive to not only the medications used to treat scabies but also often to flea-control products.

Otodectes cynotis is the canine ear mite and is one of the more common causes of mange, especially in young dogs in shelters or pet stores. That's because the mites are typically present in large numbers and are quickly spread to

Micrograph of a dog louse, *Heterodoxus spiniger*. Female lice attach their eggs to the hairs of the dog. As the eggs hatch, the larval lice bite and feed on the blood. Lice can also feed on dead skin and hair. This feeding activity can cause hair loss and skin problems.

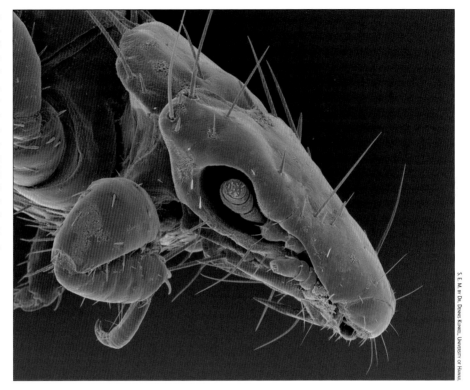

S. E. M. BY DR. DENNIS KUNKEL, UNIVERSITY OF HAWAII

nearby animals. The mites rarely do much harm but can be difficult to eradicate if the treatment regimen is not comprehensive. While many try to treat the condition with ear drops only, this is the most common cause of treatment failure. Ear drops cause the mites to simply move out of the ears and as far away as possible (usually to the base of the tail) until the insecticide levels in the ears drop to an acceptable level—then it's back to business as usual! The successful treatment of ear mites requires treating all animals in the household with a systemic insecti-

cide, such as selamectin, or a combination of miticidal ear drops combined with whole-body flea-control preparations.

Demodicosis, sometimes referred to as red mange, can be one of the most difficult forms of mange to treat. Part of the problem has to do with the fact that the mites live in the hair follicles and they are relatively well shielded from topical and systemic products. The main issue, however, is that demodectic mange typically results only when there is some underlying process interfering with the dog's immune system.

Since *Demodex* mites are normal residents of the skin of mammals, including humans, there is usually a mite population explosion only when the immune system fails to keep the number of mites in check. In young animals, the immune deficit may be transient or may reflect an actual inherited immune problem. In older animals, demodicosis is usually seen only when there is another disease hampering the immune system, such as diabetes, cancer, thyroid problems or the use of immune-suppressing drugs. Accordingly, treatment involves not only trying to kill the mange mites but also discerning what is interfering with immune function and correcting it if possible.

Chiggers represent several different species of mite that don't parasitize dogs specifically, but do latch on to passersby and can cause irritation. The problem is most prevalent in wooded areas in the late summer and fall. Treatment is not difficult, as the mites do not complete their life cycle on dogs and are susceptible to a variety of miticidal products.

MOSQUITOES

Mosquitoes have long been known to transmit a variety of diseases to people, as well as just being biting pests during warm weather. They also pose a real risk to pets. Not only do they carry deadly heartworms but recently there also has been much concern over their involvement with West Nile virus. While we can avoid heartworm with the use of preventive medications, there are no such preventives for West Nile virus. The only method of prevention in endemic areas is active mosquito control. Fortunately, most dogs that have been exposed to the virus only developed flu-like symptoms and, to date, there have not been the large number of reported deaths in canines as seen in some other species.

ILLUSTRATION BY PHOTOTAKE

Illustration of *Demodex folliculoram.*

MOSQUITO REPELLENT

Low concentrations of DEET (less than 10%), found in many human mosquito repellents, have been safely used in dogs but, in these concentrations, probably give only about two hours of protection. DEET may be safe in these small concentrations, but since it is not licensed for use on dogs, there is no research proving its safety for dogs. Products containing permethrin give the longest-lasting protection, perhaps two to four weeks. As DEET is not licensed for use on dogs, and both DEET and permethrin can be quite toxic to cats, appropriate care should be exercised. Other products, such as those containing oil of citronella, also have some mosquito-repellent activity, but typically have a relatively short duration of action.

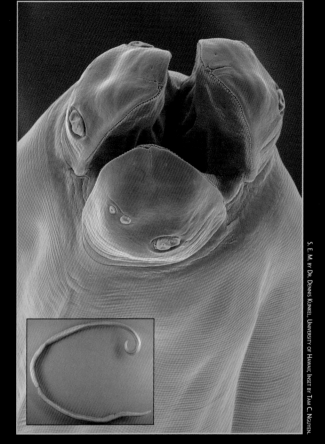

S. E. M. BY DR. DENNIS KUNKEL, UNIVERSITY OF HAWAII. INSET BY TAM C. NGUYEN.

The ascarid roundworm Toxocara canis, *showing the mouth with three lips. INSET: Photomicrograph of the roundworm* Ascaris lumbricoides.

INTERNAL PARASITES: WORMS

ASCARIDS

Ascarids are intestinal roundworms that rarely cause severe disease in dogs. Nonetheless, they are of major public health significance because they can be transferred to people. Sadly, it is children who are most commonly affected by the parasite, probably from inadvertently ingesting ascarid-contaminated soil. In fact, many yards and children's sandboxes contain appreciable numbers of ascarid eggs. So, while ascarids don't bite dogs or latch onto their intestines to suck blood, they do cause some nasty medical conditions in children and are best eradicated from our furry friends. Because pups can start passing ascarid eggs by three weeks of age, most parasite-control programs begin at two weeks of age and are repeated every two weeks until pups are eight weeks old. It is important to

S. E. M. BY DR. DENNIS KUNKEL, UNIVERSITY OF HAWAII.

realize that bitches can pass ascarids to their pups even if they test negative prior to whelping. Accordingly, bitches are best treated at the same time as the pups.

HOOKWORMS

Unlike ascarids, hookworms do latch onto a dog's intestinal tract and can cause significant loss of blood and protein. Similar to ascarids, hookworms can be transmitted to humans, where they cause a condition known as cutaneous larval migrans. Dogs can become infected either by consuming the infective larvae or by the larvae's penetrating the skin directly. People most often get infected when they are lying on the ground (such as on a beach) and the larvae penetrate the skin. Yes, the larvae can penetrate through a beach blanket. Hookworms are typically susceptible to the same medications used to treat ascarids.

The hookworm *Ancylostoma caninum* infests the intestines of dogs. INSET: Note the row of hooks at the posterior end, used to anchor the worm to the intestinal wall.

WHIPWORMS

Whipworms latch onto the lower aspects of the dog's colon and can cause cramping and diarrhea. Eggs do not start to appear in the dog's feces until about three months after the dog was infected. This worm has a peculiar life cycle, which makes it more difficult to control than ascarids or hookworms. The good thing is that whipworms rarely are transferred to people.

Some of the medications used to treat ascarids and hookworms are also effective against whipworms, but, in general, a separate treatment protocol is needed. Since most of the medications are effective against the adults but not the eggs or larvae, treatment is typically repeated in three weeks, and then often in three

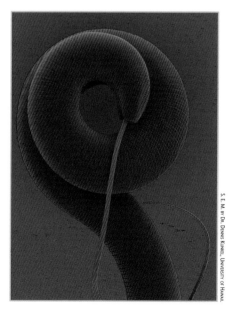

Adult whipworm, *Trichuris* sp., an intestinal parasite.

S. E. M. by Dr. Dennis Kunkel, University of Hawaii.

> ## WORM-CONTROL GUIDELINES
> - Practice sanitary habits with your dog and home.
> - Clean up after your dog and don't let him sniff or eat other dogs' droppings.
> - Control insects and fleas in the dog's environment. Fleas, lice, cockroaches, beetles, mice and rats can act as hosts for various worms.
> - Prevent dogs from eating uncooked meat, raw poultry and dead animals.
> - Keep dogs and children from playing in sand and soil.
> - Kennel dogs on cement or gravel; avoid dirt runs.
> - Administer heartworm preventives regularly.
> - Have your vet examine your dog's stools at your annual visits.
> - Select a boarding kennel carefully so as to avoid contamination from other dogs or an unsanitary environment.
> - Prevent dogs from roaming. Obey local leash laws.

months as well. Unfortunately, since dogs don't develop resistance to whipworms, it is difficult to prevent them from getting reinfected if they visit soil contaminated with whipworm eggs.

TAPEWORMS

There are many different species of tapeworm that affect dogs, but *Dipylidium caninum* is probably the most common and is spread by fleas. Flea larvae feed on organic debris and tapeworm eggs in the environment and, when a dog chews at himself and manages to ingest fleas, he might get a dose of tapeworm at the same time. The tapeworm then develops further in the intestine of the dog.

The tapeworm itself, which is a parasitic flatworm that latches onto the intestinal wall, is composed of numerous segments. When the segments break off into the intestine (as proglottids), they may accumulate around the rectum, like grains of rice. While this tapeworm is disgusting in its behavior, it is not directly communicable to humans (although humans can also get infected by swallowing fleas).

A much more dangerous flatworm is *Echinococcus multilocularis*, which is typically found in foxes, coyotes and wolves. The eggs are passed in the feces and infect rodents, and, when dogs eat the rodents, the dogs can be infected by thousands of adult tapeworms. While the parasites don't cause many problems in dogs, this is considered the most lethal worm infection that people can get. Take appropriate precautions if you live in an area in which these tapeworms are found. Do not use mulch that may contain feces of dogs, cats or wildlife, and

discourage your pets from hunting wildlife. Treat these tapeworm infections aggressively in pets, because if humans get infected, approximately half die.

HEARTWORMS

Heartworm disease is caused by the parasite *Dirofilaria immitis* and is seen in dogs around the world. A member of the roundworm group, it is spread between dogs by the bite of an infected mosquito. The mosquito injects infective larvae into the dog's skin with its bite, and these larvae develop under the skin for a period of time before making their way to the heart. There they develop into adults, which grow and create blockages of the heart, lungs and major blood vessels there. They also start producing offspring (microfilariae),

A dog tapeworm proglottid (body segment).

The dog tapeworm *Taenia pisiformis*.

A Look at Internal Parasites

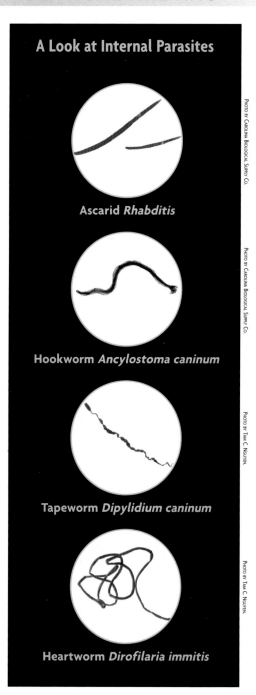

Ascarid *Rhabditis*

Photo by Carolina Biological Supply Co.

Hookworm *Ancylostoma caninum*

Photo by Carolina Biological Supply Co.

Tapeworm *Dipylidium caninum*

Photo by Tam C. Nguyen.

Heartworm *Dirofilaria immitis*

Photo by Tam C. Nguyen.

and these microfilariae circulate in the bloodstream, waiting to hitch a ride when the next mosquito bites. Once in the mosquito, the microfilariae develop into infective larvae and the entire process is repeated.

When dogs get infected with heartworm, over time they tend to develop symptoms associated with heart disease, such as coughing, exercise intolerance and potentially many other manifestations. Diagnosis is confirmed by either seeing the microfilariae themselves in blood samples or using immunologic tests (antigen testing) to identify the presence of adult heartworms. Since antigen tests measure the presence of adult heartworms and microfilarial tests measure offspring produced by adults, neither are positive until six to seven months after the initial infection. However, the beginning of damage can occur by fifth-stage larvae as early as three months after infection. Thus it is possible for dogs to be harboring problem-causing larvae for up to three months before either type of test would identify an infection.

The good news is that there are great protocols available for preventing heartworm in dogs. Testing is critical in the process, and it is important to understand the benefits as well as the limitations of such testing. All dogs six months of age or older that have not been on continuous heartworm-preventive medication should be

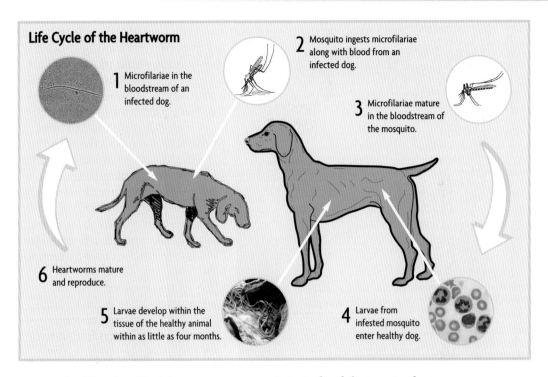

Life Cycle of the Heartworm

1 Microfilariae in the bloodstream of an infected dog.

2 Mosquito ingests microfilariae along with blood from an infected dog.

3 Microfilariae mature in the bloodstream of the mosquito.

4 Larvae from infested mosquito enter healthy dog.

5 Larvae develop within the tissue of the healthy animal within as little as four months.

6 Heartworms mature and reproduce.

screened with microfilarial or antigen tests. For dogs receiving preventive medication, periodic antigen testing helps assess the effectiveness of the preventives. The American Heartworm Society guidelines suggest that annual retesting may not be necessary when owners have absolutely provided continuous heartworm prevention. Retesting on a two- to three-year interval may be sufficient in these cases. However, your veterinarian will likely have specific guidelines under which heartworm preventives will be prescribed, and many prefer to err on the side of safety and retest annually.

It is indeed fortunate that heartworm is relatively easy to prevent, because treatments can be as life-threatening as the disease itself. Treatment requires a two-step process that kills the adult heartworms first and then the microfilariae. Prevention is obviously preferable; this involves a once-monthly oral or topical treatment. The most common oral preventives include ivermectin (not suitable for some breeds), moxidectin and milbemycin oxime; the once-a-month topical drug selamectin provides heartworm protection in addition to flea, tick and other parasite controls.

Is dog showing in your blood? Are you excited by the idea of gaiting your handsome Spinone around the ring to the thunderous applause of an enthusiastic audience? Are you certain that your beloved Spinone is flawless? You are not alone! Every loving owner thinks that his dog has no faults, or too few to mention. No matter how many times an owner reads the breed standard, he cannot find any faults in his aristo-cratic companion dog. If this sounds like you, and if you are considering entering your Spinone in a dog show, here are some basic questions to ask yourself:

If you have selected a Spinone with the intentions of showing him, begin teaching him to stand stock still for inspection. Pointing pups do this quite instinctively.

- Did you purchase a "show-quality" puppy from the breeder?
- Is your puppy at least six months of age?
- Does the puppy exhibit correct show type for his breed?
- Does your puppy have any disqualifying faults?
- Is your Spinone registered with the American Kennel Club?
- How much time do you have to devote to training, grooming, conditioning and exhibiting your dog?
- Do you understand the rules and regulations of a dog show?
- Do you have time to learn how to show your dog properly?
- Do you have the financial resources to invest in showing your dog?
- Will you show the dog yourself or hire a professional handler?
- Do you have a vehicle that can accommodate your weekend trips to the dog shows?

Success in the show ring requires more than a pretty face, a waggy tail and a pocketful of liver. Even though dog shows can be exciting and enjoyable, the sport of conformation makes great demands on the exhibitors and the dogs. Winning exhibitors live for

their dogs, devoting time and money to their dogs' presentation, conditioning and training. Very few novices, even those with good dogs, will find themselves in the winners' circle, though it does happen. Don't be disheartened. Every exhibitor began as a novice and worked his way up to the Group ring. It's the "working your way up" part that you must keep in mind.

Assuming that you have purchased a puppy of the correct type and quality for showing, let's begin to examine the world of showing and what's required to get started. Although the entry fee into a dog show is nominal, there are lots of other hidden costs involved with "finishing" your Spinone, that is, making him a champion. Things like equipment, travel, training and conditioning all cost money. A more serious campaign will include fees for a professional handler, boarding, cross-country travel and advertising. Top-winning show dogs can represent a very considerable investment—over $100,000 has been spent in campaigning some dogs. (The investment can be less, of course, for owners who don't use professional handlers.)

Many owners, on the other hand, enter their "average" Spinoni in dog shows for the fun and enjoyment of it. Dog showing makes an absorbing hobby, with many rewards for dogs and owners

FOR MORE INFORMATION...
For reliable up-to-date information about registration, dog shows and other canine competitions, contact one of the national registries by mail or via the Internet.
American Kennel Club
5580 Centerview Dr., Raleigh, NC 27606-3390
www.akc.org

United Kennel Club
100 E. Kilgore Road, Kalamazoo, MI 49002
www.ukcdogs.com

Canadian Kennel Club
89 Skyway Ave., Suite 100, Etobicoke, Ontario M9W 6R4 Canada
www.ckc.ca

The Kennel Club
1-5 Clarges St., Piccadilly, London W1Y 8AB, UK
www.the-kennel-club.org.uk

alike. If you're having fun, meeting other people who share your interests and enjoying the overall experience, you likely will catch the "bug." Once the dog-show bug bites, its effects can last a lifetime; it's certainly much better than a deer tick! Soon you will be envisioning yourself in the center ring at the Westminster Kennel Club Dog Show in New York City, competing for the prestigious Best in Show cup. This magical dog show is televised annually from Madison Square Garden, and the victorious dog becomes a celebrity overnight.

group compete against each other; this is done for all seven groups. Finally, all seven group winners go head to head in the ring for the Best in Show award.

What most spectators don't understand is the basic idea of conformation. A dog show is often referred to as a "conformation" show. This means that the judge should decide how each dog stacks up (conforms) to the breed standard for his given breed: how well does this Spinone conform to the ideal representative detailed in the standard? Ideally, this is what happens. In reality, however, this ideal often gets slighted as the judge compares Spinone #1 to Spinone #2. Again, the ideal is that each dog is judged based on his merits in comparison to his breed standard, not in comparison to the other dogs in the ring. It is easier for judges to compare dogs of the same breed to decide which they think is the better specimen; in the Group and Best in Show ring, however, it is very difficult to compare one breed to another, like apples to oranges. Thus the dog's conformation to the breed standard—not to mention advertising dollars and good handling—is essential to success in conformation shows. The dog described in the standard (the standard for each AKC breed is written and approved by the breed's national parent club and then submitted to the AKC for

The handler "stacks" or "stands" the dog in the show ring. A sure way to keep him in position is to focus his attention on a tasty tidbit.

AKC CONFORMATION SHOWING

GETTING STARTED

Visiting a dog show as a spectator is a great place to start. Pick up the show catalog to find out what time your breed is being shown, who is judging the breed and in which ring the classes will be held. To start, Spinoni compete against other Spinoni, and the winner is selected as Best of Breed by the judge. This is the procedure for each breed. At a group show, all of the Best of Breed winners go on to compete for Group One in their respective groups. For example, all Best of Breed winners in a given

approval) is the perfect dog of that breed, and breeders keep their eye on the standard when they choose which dogs to breed, hoping to get closer and closer to the elusive ideal with each litter.

Another good first step for the novice is to join a dog club. You will be astonished by the many and different kinds of dog clubs in the country, with about 5,000 clubs holding events every year. Most clubs require that prospective new members present two letters of recommendation from existing members. Perhaps you've made some friends visiting a show held by a particular club and you would like to join that club. Dog clubs may specialize in a single breed, like a local or regional Spinone club, or in a specific pursuit, such as obedience, tracking or hunting tests. There are all-breed clubs for all dog enthusiasts; they sponsor special training days, seminars on topics like grooming or handling or lectures on breeding or canine genetics. There are also clubs that specialize in certain types of dogs, like hunting dogs, herding dogs, companion dogs, etc.

A parent club is the national organization, sanctioned by the AKC, which promotes and safeguards its breed in the country. The Spinone Italiano Club of America was formed in 2000 and can be contacted on the Internet at www.spinone.com. The parent club holds an annual national specialty show, usually in a different city each year, in which many of the country's top dogs, handlers and breeders gather to compete. At a specialty show, only members of a single breed are invited to participate. There are also group specialties, in which all members of a group are invited. For more information about dog clubs in your area, contact the AKC at www.akc.org on the Internet or write them at their Raleigh, NC address.

HOW SHOWS ARE ORGANIZED
Three kinds of conformation shows are offered by the AKC. There is the all-breed show, in which all AKC-recognized breeds can compete; the specialty show,

Showing your Spinone is a wonderful activity for owner and dog alike. Conformation shows bring new challenges and rewards for dogs and fanciers.

which is for one breed only and usually sponsored by the breed's parent club and the group show, for all breeds in one of the AKC's seven groups. The Spinone Italiano competes in the Sporting Group.

For a dog to become an AKC champion of record, the dog must earn 15 points at shows. The points must be awarded by at least three different judges and must include two "majors" under different judges. A "major" is a three-, four- or five-point win, and the number of points per win is determined by the number of dogs competing in the show on that day. (Dogs that are absent or are excused are not counted.) The number of points that are awarded varies from breed to breed. More dogs are needed to attain a major in more popular breeds, and fewer dogs are needed in less popular breeds. Yearly, the AKC evaluates the number of dogs in competition in each division (there are 14 divisions in all, based on geography) and may or may not change the numbers of dogs required for each number of points. For example, a major in Division 2 (Delaware, New Jersey and Pennsylvania) recently required 17 dogs or 16 bitches for a three-point major, 29 dogs or 27 bitches for a four-point major and 51 dogs or 46 bitches for a five-point major. The Spinone attracts numerically proportionate representation at all-breed shows.

Only one dog and one bitch of each breed can win points at a given show. There are no "co-ed" classes except for champions of record. Dogs and bitches do not compete against each other until they are champions. Dogs that are not champions (referred to as "class dogs") compete in one of five classes. The class in which a dog is entered depends on age and previous show wins. First there is the Puppy Class (sometimes divided further into classes for 6- to 9-month-olds and 9- to 12-month-olds); next is the Novice Class (for dogs that have no points toward their championship and whose only first-place wins have come in the Puppy Class or the Novice Class, the latter class limited to three first places); then there is the American-bred Class (for dogs bred in the US); the Bred-by-Exhibitor Class (for dogs handled by their breeders or by immediate family members of their breeders) and the Open Class (for any non-champions). Any dog may enter the Open Class, regardless of age or win history, but to be competitive the dog should be older and have ring experience.

The judge at the show begins judging the male dogs in the Puppy Class(es) and proceeds through the other classes. The judge awards first through fourth place in each class. The first-place winners of each class then compete with one another in the Winners Class to determine Winners Dog. The judge then starts over with the bitches, beginning with the Puppy Class(es) and proceeding up to the Winners Class to award Winners Bitch, just as he did with the dogs. A Reserve Winners Dog and Reserve Winners Bitch are also selected; they could be awarded the points in the case of a disqualification.

The Winners Dog and Winners Bitch are the two that are awarded the points for their breed. They then go on to compete with any champions of record (often called "specials") of their breed that are entered in the show. The champions may be dogs or bitches; in this class, all are shown together. The judge reviews the Winners Dog and Winners Bitch along with all of the champions to select the Best of Breed winner. The Best of Winners is selected between the Winners Dog and Winners Bitch; if one of these two is selected Best of Breed as well, he or she is automatically determined Best of Winners. Lastly, the judge selects Best of Opposite Sex to the Best of Breed winner. The Best of Breed winner then goes on to the group competition.

At a group or all-breed show, the Best of Breed winners from each breed are divided into their respective groups to compete against one another for Group One

through Group Four. Group One (first place) is awarded to the dog that best lives up to the ideal for his breed as described in the standard. A group judge, therefore, must have a thorough working knowledge of many breed standards. After placements have been made in each group, the seven Group One winners (from the Sporting Group, Toy Group, Hound Group, etc.) compete against each other for the top honor, Best in Show.

There are different ways to find out about dog shows in your area. The American Kennel Club's monthly magazine, the *American Kennel Gazette* is accompanied by the *Events Calendar*; this magazine is available through subscription. You can also look on the AKC's and your parent club's websites for information and check the event listings in your local newspaper.

Your Spinone must be six

The Spinone's function, the essence of the breed, should never be lost in show dogs. It's a wonderful sight to watch this Sporting Group dog show his powerful gait in the ring.

months of age or older and
registered with the American
Kennel Club in order to be entered
in AKC-sanctioned shows in
which there are classes for the
Spinone. Your Spinone also must
not possess any disqualifying
faults and must be sexually intact.
The reason for the latter is simple:
dog shows are the proving grounds
to determine which dogs and
bitches are worthy of being bred. If
they cannot be bred, that defeats
the purpose! On that note, only
dogs that have achieved championships, thus proving their
excellent quality, should be bred. If
you have spayed or neutered your
dog, however, there are many AKC
events other than conformation,
such as obedience trials, agility
trials and the Canine Good
Citizen® Program, in which you
and your Spinone can participate.

OTHER TYPES OF COMPETITION

In addition to conformation shows,
the AKC holds a variety of other
competitive events. Obedience
trials, agility trials and tracking
trials are open to all breeds, while
hunting tests, field trials, lure
coursing, herding tests and trials,
earthdog tests and coonhound
events are limited to specific
breeds or groups of breeds. The
Junior Showmanship program is
offered to aspiring young handlers
and their dogs, and the Canine
Good Citizen® Program is an all-

around good-behavior test open to
all dogs, pure-bred and mixed.

OBEDIENCE TRIALS

Mrs. Helen Whitehouse Walker, a
Standard Poodle fancier, can be
credited with introducing
obedience trials to the United
States. In the 1930s she designed a
series of exercises based on those
of the Associated Sheep, Police,
Army Dog Society of Great Britain.
These exercises were intended to
evaluate the working relationship
between dog and owner. Since
those early days of the sport in the
US, obedience trials have grown
more and more popular, and now
more than 2,000 trials each year
attract over 100,000 dogs and their
owners. Any dog registered with
the AKC, regardless of neutering or
other disqualifications that would
preclude entry in conformation
competition, can participate in
obedience trials.

There are three levels of
difficulty in obedience competition. The first (and easiest) level is
the Novice, in which dogs can
earn the Companion Dog (CD) title.

AKC GROUPS

For showing purposes, the American
Kennel Club divides its recognized
breeds into seven groups: Sporting
Dogs, Hounds, Working Dogs,
Terriers, Toys, Non-Sporting Dogs
and Herding Dogs.

Doin' what comes naturally, here's Ch. Dee Tias Julius Pleaser JH, owned by Michelle and Lauren Brustein and Dave Brooks, taking Best in Show.

The intermediate level is the Open level, in which the Companion Dog Excellent (CDX) title is awarded. The advanced level is the Utility level, in which dogs compete for the Utility Dog (UD) title. Classes at each level are further divided into "A" and "B," with "A" for beginners and "B" for those with more experience. In order to win a title at a given level, a dog must earn three "legs." A "leg" is accomplished when a dog scores 170 or higher (200 is a perfect score). The scoring system gets a little trickier when you understand that a dog must score more than 50% of the points available for each exercise in order to actually earn the points. Available points for each exercise range between 20 and 40.

A dog must complete different exercises at each level of obedience. The Novice exercises are the easiest, with the Open and finally the Utility levels progressing in difficulty. Examples of Novice exercises are on- and off-lead heeling, a figure-8 pattern, performing a recall (or come), long sit and long down and standing for examination. In the Open level, the Novice-level exercises are required again, but this time without a leash and for longer durations. In addition, the dog must clear a broad jump, retrieve over a jump and drop on recall. In the Utility level, the exercises are quite difficult, including executing basic commands based on hand signals, following a complex heeling pattern, locating articles based on scent discrimination and completing jumps at the handler's direction.

Once he's earned the UD title, a dog can go on to win the prestigious title of Utility Dog Excellent (UDX) by winning "legs" in ten shows. Additionally, Utility Dogs who win "legs" in Open B and Utility B earn points toward the lofty title of Obedience Trial Champion (OTCh.). Established in 1977 by the AKC, this title requires a dog to earn 100 points as well as three first places in a combination of Open B and Utility B classes under three different judges. The "brass ring" of obedience competition is the AKC's National Obedience Invitational. This is an exclusive competition for only the cream of the obedience crop. In order to qualify for the invitational, a dog must be ranked in either the top 25 all-breeds in obedience or in the top three for his breed in obedience. The title at stake here is that of National Obedience Champion (NOC).

AGILITY TRIALS

Agility trials became sanctioned by the AKC in August 1994, when the first licensed agility trials were held. Since that time, agility certainly has grown in popularity by leaps and bounds, literally! The AKC allows all registered breeds (including Miscellaneous Class breeds) to participate, providing the dog is 12 months of age or older. Agility is designed so that the handler demonstrates how well the dog can work at his side. The handler directs his dog through, over, under and around an obstacle course that includes jumps, tires, the dog walk, weave poles, pipe tunnels, collapsed tunnels and more. While working his way through the course, the dog must keep one eye and ear on the handler and the rest of his body on the course. The handler runs along with the dog, giving verbal and hand signals to guide the dog through the course.

The first organization to promote agility trials in the US was the United States Dog Agility Association, Inc. (USDAA). Established in 1986, the USDAA sparked the formation of many member clubs around the country. To participate in USDAA trials, dogs must be at least 18 months of age.

The USDAA and AKC both offer titles to winning dogs, although the exercises and requirements of the two organizations differ. Agility Dog (AD), Advanced Agility Dog (AAD) and Master Agility Dog (MAD) are the titles offered by the USDAA, while the AKC offers Novice Agility (NA),

FIELD AND GUNDOG WORK

Most Spinoni excel at the business of finding and retrieving game—hunting! A well-trained Spinone, a pointer by trade, is a joy on rough shoots and an asset when picking up behind the guns.

When picking up, the dog and the handler are assigned an area to cover and clear of birds. The dogs push out the game as well as retrieve the fallen birds. Working in a natural environment with his instincts in high gear, the Spinone can revel in his natural heritage and clearly enjoys every working minute.

In rough shooting, the dog and handler work alone as a single team, hunting, shooting and retrieving game. The dogs visibly love their job, and their owners enjoy seeing the dogs work as much as, if not more than, the actual shoot. A Spinone can work in the field until around six years of age, which is an impressive field career for any dog.

Open Agility (OA), Agility Excellent (AX) and Master Agility Excellent (MX). Beyond these four AKC titles, dogs can win additional titles in "jumper" classes: Jumper with Weave Novice (NAJ), Open (OAJ) and Excellent (MXJ). The ultimate title in AKC agility is MACH, Master Agility Champion. Dogs can continue to add number designations to the MACH title, indicating how many times the dog has met the title's requirements (MACH1, MACH2 and so on).

Agility trials are a great way to keep your dog active, and they will keep you running, too! You should join a local agility club to learn more about the sport. These clubs offer sessions in which you can introduce your dog to the various obstacles as well as training classes to prepare him for competition. In no time, your dog will be climbing A-frames, crossing the dog walk and flying over hurdles, all with you right beside him. Your heart will leap every time your dog jumps through the hoop—and you'll be having just as much (if not more) fun!

TRACKING

Tracking tests are exciting ways to test your Spinone's instinctive scenting ability on a competitive level. All dogs have a nose, and all breeds are welcome in tracking tests. The first AKC-licensed tracking test took place in 1937 as part of the Utility level at an obedience trial, and thus competitive tracking was officially begun. The first title, Tracking Dog (TD), was offered in 1947, ten years after the first official tracking test. It was not until 1980 that the AKC added the title Tracking Dog Excellent (TDX), which was followed by the title Versatile Surface Tracking (VST) in 1995. Champion Tracker (CT) is awarded to a dog who has earned all three of those titles.

The TD level is the first and most basic level in tracking, progressing in difficulty to the TDX and then the VST. A dog must follow a track laid by a human 30 to 120 minutes prior in order to earn the TD title. The track is about 500 yards long and contains up to 5 directional changes. At the next level, the TDX, the dog must follow a 3- to 5-hour-old track over a course that is up to 1,000 yards long and has up to 7 directional changes. In the most difficult level, the VST, the track is up to five hours old and located in an urban setting.

FIELD TRIALS

Field trials are offered to the retrievers, pointers (which includes the Spinone) and spaniel breeds of the Sporting Group as well as to the Beagles, Dachshunds

Hunting is in the Spinone's blood. Here's an expert flusher and retriever.

MEET THE AKC
The American Kennel Club is the main governing body of the dog sport in the United States. Founded in 1884, the AKC consists of 500 or more independent dog clubs plus 4,500 affiliated clubs, all of which follow the AKC rules and regulations. Additionally, the AKC maintains a registry for pure-bred dogs in the US and works to preserve the integrity of the sport and its continuation in the country. Over 1,000,000 dogs are registered each year, representing about 150 recognized breeds. There are over 15,000 competitive events held annually for which over 2,000,000 dogs enter to participate. Dogs compete to earn over 40 different titles, from Champion to Companion Dog to Master Agility Champion.

and Bassets of the Hound Group. The purpose of field trials is to demonstrate a dog's ability to perform his breed's original purpose in the field. The events vary depending on the type of dog, but in all trials dogs compete against one another for placement and for points toward their Field Champion (FC) titles. Dogs that earn their FC titles plus their championship in the conformation ring are known as Dual Champions; this is extremely prestigious, as it shows that the dog is the ideal blend of form and function, excelling in both areas.

Retriever field trials, designed to simulate "an ordinary day's shoot," are popular and likely the most demanding of these trials. Dogs must "mark" the location of downed feathered game and then return the birds to the shooter. Successful dogs are able to "mark" the downed game by remembering where the bird fell as well as correct use of the wind and terrain. Dogs are tested both on land and in water.

Difficulty levels are based on the number of birds downed as well as the number of "blind retrieves" (where a bird is placed away from the view of the dog and the handler directs the dog by the use of hand signals and verbal commands). The term "Non-Slip" retriever, often applied to these trials, refers to a dog that is steady at the handler's side until commanded to go. Every field trial includes four stakes of increasing levels of difficulty. Each stake is judged by a team of two judges who look for many natural abilities, including steadiness, courage, style, control and training.

HUNTING TESTS

Hunting tests are not competitive like field trials, and participating dogs are judged against a standard, as in a conformation show. The first hunting tests were devised by the North American Hunting Retriever Association (NAHRA) as an alternative to field trials for

retriever owners to appreciate their dogs' natural innate ability in the field without the expense and pressure of a formal field trial. The intent of hunting tests is the same as that of field trials: to test the dog's ability in a simulated hunting scenario.

The AKC instituted its hunting tests in June 1985; since then, their popularity has grown tremendously. The AKC offers three titles at hunting tests, Junior Hunter (JH), Senior Hunter (SH) and Master Hunter (MH). Each title requires that the dog earn qualifying "legs" at the tests: the JH requiring four; the SH, five; and the MH, six. In addition to the AKC, the United Kennel Club also offers hunting tests through its affiliate club, the Hunting Retriever Club, Inc. (HRC), which began holding the tests in 1984.

This Spinone and handler are participating in a hunting trial. This is perhaps the most enjoyable type of competition for this talented field dog.

INDEX

Activities 115
Adaptability 27
Adenovirus 126
Adult
—adoption 32, 92
—health 123
—training 90, 92
Advanced Agility Dog 152
Aggression 58, 93, 116, 128
Agility Dog 152
Agility Excellent 152
Agility trials 116, 150, 152
Alba del Sasso 20
All-breed show 149
Alpha role 102
American Heartworm Society 143
American Kennel Club 21-22, 116, 144, 148, 150, 154-155
—address 145
—competitive events 150
—conformation showing 146
—standard 37
American Kennel Gazette 150
American-bred Class 149
Amirian, Lena 22
Ancylostoma caninum **139**, **142**
Annual vet exams 123
Antifreeze 57
Appetite loss 121
Applegate, Ed and Suzanne 23
Arno 16
Ascarid **138**, 139
Ascaris lumbricoides **138**
Attention 103-104, 110
Backpacking 115
Ballard, Wendy 89
Bannonbrig 18
Barking 30-31
Barlow, Glenys 18
Bathing 79-80
Bedding 48, 60, 98
Behavioral problems 30
Best in Show 146, 150
Best of Breed 146, 149
Best of Opposite Sex 149
Best of Winners 149
Bevan, Cyndy and Malcolm 18
Bloat 33-35, 76, 77
Body language 93, 100
Body temperature 123
Bones 49
Bordetella bronchiseptica 126, 128
Boredom 35
Borrelia burgdorferi 126
Borreliosis 128
Bowls 46
Bracco Italiano **13**, **14**
Bracco Spinone 15
Bracco Spinoso 15
Braque d'Auvergne **13**
Braque du Bourbonnais **13**
Braque Français **13**, **14**
Braque St. Germain **13**
Bred-by-Exhibitor Class 149
Breed club 20-22, 42, 116, 147
Breed name 9, 19
Breed standard 37, 146
Breeder 33, 42, 47, 68-69, 73, 119
—selection 42, 45, 119
Brooks, Dave 22
Brushing 79-80

Brustein, Michelle and Lauren 22
Caffeine 75
Caldocani 18
Canadian Kennel Club 145
Cancer 128
Canine cerebellar ataxia 33
Canine cough 126
Canine development schedule 95
Canine Good Citizen® 150
Canis domesticus 11
Canis lupus 9, 11
Canis lupus chanco 10
Cantoni, Sergio 17
Car travel 61, 116
Careena, Mr. & Mrs. 18
Cat 32, 63
Cerebella del Caos **22**, 23
Cesky Fousek **13**
Challenge Certificates 18
Champion 148
Champion Tracker 153
Channon, Jim 22, 23
Chew toys 49, 59, 66, 97-98
Chewing 30, 35, 48, 59, 64, 116
Cheyletiella mite **135**
Chiggers 137
Children 25, 27, 59, 61, 65, 93, 115-116
Chocolate 75
Chruston 18
Class dogs 148
Classes at shows 148
Clipping 79
Club Italiano Spinoni 16
Clubs 147
Coat 79-80
Cocoa 75
Cognitive dysfunction 124
Collar 51, 53, 87, 103, 116
Collins, Mrs. Linda 18
Colombo, Giulio 14
Colors 31
Comb 79
Come 67, 109, 116
Commands 105-113
—practicing 106, 109
—potty 98
Commitment of ownership 44-45
Companion Animal Recovery 89
Companion Dog 151
Competitive events 150
Conformation 144-146, 150
Connomar Careena 18
Consistency 62, 64-65, 94, 102-103
Coonhound events 150
Core vaccines 128
Coronavirus 126, 128
Correction 30, 103
Crate 47, 59-60, 67, 97
—pad 48
Crying 60, 67, 98
Ctenocephalides canis **130**
Curgenven, Margaret and John 18
Dangers in the home 56-57
Davies, Barbara 18
Dee Tias Julius Pleaser 22, **23, 151**
DEET 137
Del Sasso 20
Deldawn 18
Deldawn Federico at Dazen 21

Demodex mite **137**
Demodicosis 136-137
Dental health 86, 121, 123
Di Morghengo 20
Dickey, Larry 20
Diet 34, 68-73
Digging 30
Dilatation 34
Dingo Group 10
Dipylidium caninum 140, **142**
Dirofilaria immitis 141, **142, 143**
Discipline 64, 67, 102
Distemper 126, 128
Dog club 42, 147
Dog News 19
Dogfight 116
DogGone™ newsletter 89
Dominance 44, 106
Down 99, 106
Down/stay 109
Drop it 115
Dry bath 79
Dual Champion 154
Ear 84
—mite 135-136
Echinococcus multilocularis 141
Ectropion 35
Enciclopedia del Cane 14
Encyclopedia of Dogs 14
Endurance 29
Energy level 25, 29, 35
England 16, 20
Ente Nazionale della Cinofilia Italiano 16
Entropion 35
Estrus 128, 129
Events Calendar 150
Excessive drinking 76
Exercise 24, 29, 34-35, 77
—pen 97
—puppy 78
Expenses of ownership 50
Expression 28
External parasites 130-137
Eye care 85
Eye problems 35
Family meeting the puppy 56, 59
Family dog 27, 30
Fats 73
Fear 58
—period 62
Fédération Cynologique Interna-tionale 14
Feeding 34, 68-76
Feinnes, Richard and Alice 10
Fenced yard 57, 116
Fendley, Pat 22
Field Champion 154
Field trials 18, 115, 150, 154
Field work 35
Fiorone, Fiorenzo 14
First night in new home 60
Fleas **130**, 131, **132**
Food 28, 34, 68, 97
—bowls 46
—loss of interest in 121
—maintenance 69
—puppy 69
—rewards 91, 103, 108, 112-113
—stealing 29
—types 69, 74
Friz del Odivane 17
Gadsby, Michael 18

Gaesten 18
Gallowdyke Pawnee 18
Gallowdyke Wreckless Eric at Sundeala 18
Gastric torsion 33-34, 77
Gastroplexy 34
Gender differences 30, 44
Genetic testing 119
German Shorthaired Pointer 14
Gern, Chuck 22
Getting started in showing 146
Giardia 126
Gita 16
Give it 115
Gray wolf **11**
Greece, ancient 11
Greyhound Group 10
Grinder for nails 84
Grooming 27, 79, 84
—equipment 79, 81
Group competition 146, 149
Gum disease 121
Gundog work 153
Gundog Working Certificate 18
Gundogs 11
Handler 144
Hanna, Ed 23
Health
—benefits of dog ownership 25
—concerns 32
—insurance 57, 127
—journal 58
Heart disease 123
Heartworm 121, 141, **142, 143**
Heat cycle 128-129
Heel 111, 113
Height 30
Hepatitis 126, 128
Herding events 150
Heterodoxus spiniger **136**
Hip dysplasia 33
HomeAgain™ Companion Animal Retrieval System 89
Homemade toys 53
Hookworm **139**, **142**
Hot spots 79
Houltram, Jean 18
Hounds 11
House Guardian Dogs 10
House-training 47, 65, 94, 97-99
—puppy needs 96
—schedule 100-101
Hunger 28, 68-69
Hunting 29, 153
—ability 14, 36, 116
—dog 11, 18, 24, 32, 36
—tests 150, 155
Hunting Retriever Club 155
Hutchinson's Dog Encyclopedia 18, 21
Identification 87-88
Infectious diseases 127
Insurance 127
Intelligence 27, 29
Internal parasites 138-143
Isis La Dolce Vita 22
Iso Dell'Adige 21
Italian pointers 14
Italian Spinone Club of Great Britain 17
Italy 11, 19
Ixodes dammini **133-134**
Judge 37, 148-149

My Spinone Italiano

PUT YOUR PUPPY'S FIRST PICTURE HERE

Dog's Name _____

Date _____ Photographer _____